MW00452383

SEEING JESUS

IN UNEXPECTED PLACES

A FASCINATING LOOK AT THE
OLD TESTAMENT TABERNACLE

ADRIAN ROGERS

innovo
PUBLISHING

Published by Innovo Publishing, LLC
www.innovopublishing.com
1-888-546-2111

Providing Full-Service Publishing Services for Christian Authors, Artists &
Ministries: Books, eBooks, Audiobooks, Music, Screenplays, Film & Curricula

SEEING JESUS IN UNEXPECTED PLACES
A Fascinating Look at the Old Testament Tabernacle

ISBN: 978-1-61314-872-3

Cover Design: Jeff Hatcher
Interior Layout: Innovo Publishing, LLC
Printed in the United States of America
U.S. Printing History
First Edition: 2022

Has God called you to create a Christian book, eBook, audiobook, music album,
screenplay, film, or curricula? If so, visit the ChristianPublishingPortal.com to
learn how to accomplish your calling with excellence. Learn to do everything
yourself, or hire trusted Christian Experts from our Marketplace to help.

CONTENTS

INTRODUCTION

Where Will You See Jesus?

The story of Jesus is found throughout the whole Bible. The Gospel of Jesus Christ is communicated in the entirety of God's Word: Old Testament and New Testament, from Genesis to Revelation.

In the Old Testament, God repeatedly pointed to the coming Messiah. You find Him in the Garden in Genesis 3:15 as the Seed who will bruise Satan's head. He is the ark of salvation carrying Noah and his family to salvation. He is caught in a thicket at Mount Moriah in Genesis 22 as the substitute sacrifice. He is there in the lamb's blood on the doorposts in the Israelites' quarters of Egypt in Exodus 12, taking on Himself the destruction of the oldest son as the angel of death passes over God's people.

But did you know you will also find Him in the tabernacle. The portable worship center the Israelites carted through the desert was also part classroom where God taught the people of God about the coming Messiah and all He would accomplish.

In this book based on a series of messages, Adrian Rogers pulls back the curtain to reveal the details about the tabernacle that point to our Lord and Savior Jesus Christ. Chapter by chapter, you will see Him in every room and in every artifact. You'll learn more about how to worship Him in spirit and in truth. And you'll learn to always look for Jesus in unexpected places.

CHAPTER ONE

Camping with God: An Overview of the Tabernacle

To come to Jesus, you must come through Him.
—Adrian Rogers

A s we begin our study of the tabernacle, it may help for you to get a picture in your mind of what it may have been like. I heard one man describe it as, "Camping with God." In essence, the Tabernacle was a sanctuary for the Jews while they were in the wilderness.

Let's discover a little more about this sanctuary by reading Exodus 25:1-9. In this first chapter, we will learn about the tabernacle in the broadest sense. Then, in each of the next twelve chapters, we will look at more specific details about God's desert home.

Then the LORD spoke to Moses, saying: "Speak to the children of Israel, that they bring Me an offering. From everyone who gives it willingly with his heart you shall take My offering. And this is the offering which you shall take from them: gold, silver, and bronze; blue, purple, and scarlet thread, fine linen, and goats' hair; ram skins dyed red, badger skins, and acacia wood; oil for the light, and spices for the anointing oil and for the sweet incense; onyx stones, and stones to be set in the ephod and in the breastplate. And let them make Me a sanctuary, that I may dwell among them. According to all that I show you, that is, the pattern of the tabernacle and the pattern of all its furnishings, just so you shall make it.

These verses remind us that God says, "Stick to the plans. I'm going to show you precisely how I want you to make this sanctuary. The pattern is very important." Also notice the words of Exodus 25:40, "And see to it that you make them according to the pattern which was shown you on the mountain."

God reiterates. He repeats things when He wants to emphasize them. The words, "Make them according to the pattern," are important because they teach a spiritual lesson. You will see that God's precise pattern for the tabernacle in the Old Testament pointed to Jesus Christ.

Consider the words of Hebrews 8:1-2, "Now this is the main point of the things we are saying: We have such a High Priest, who is seated at the right hand of the throne of the Majesty in the heavens, a Minister of the sanctuary and of the true tabernacle which the Lord erected, and not man."

In the Old Testament, the high priest was a prophecy of our High Priest, Jesus. Hebrews 8 tells us that Jesus was and is, "a Minister of the sanctuary and of the true tabernacle which the Lord erected, and not man." Therefore, we look at the things that are happening in the Old Testament and note that they are but shadows, types, prophecies, pictures, predictions, illustrations, amplifications, and things that point to great spiritual truth in the New Testament. So many of these Old Testament symbols point us to incredible New Testament truths.

So, pay close attention as we journey through this study of the tabernacle.

The Dimensions of the Tabernacle

The tabernacle consisted of three parts: an outer court, and within that an inner court, and within that the Holy of Holies.

The outer court was 75 feet by 150 feet in size. Most average homes are built on a lot about this size. Additionally, the outer court had a fence around it. The fence was 7½ feet high. The outer court of the tabernacle had a gate that faced toward the east. This gate was very wide; it stood 30 feet across to represent that the way to God was wide open for all to enter.

In this outer court there were two pieces of furniture. First, there was a brazen altar (also called a bronze or brass altar) and there was a laver. The laver was a great basin that people washed in. The word "lave" means to bathe. In our society, we sometimes use the word lavatory to denote a bathroom or a place to bathe.

Within the outer court was a tent-like structure called the inner court that was 15 feet wide, 15 feet high, and 45 feet long. The front part of the inner court was 15 feet wide, 15 feet high, and 30 feet long. It was twice as long as it was high or wide—in it were three pieces of furniture. On the north, there was a table. To the south, there was a lampstand known as a menorah. In the rear right in the center was an altar called the altar of incense.

Finally, behind the front part of the inner court was another very small room. It was 15 feet by 15 feet by 15 feet. This room formed a perfect square—a cube. Within this room, called the Holy of Holies, were two pieces of furniture: the Ark of the Covenant and the mercy seat of God.

In future chapters, we will explain what all of these rooms and pieces of furniture signify. For now, let's look at three basic truths about the tabernacle.

First Basic Truth: The Tabernacle is a Description of Deity

The tabernacle is a description of Jesus Christ.

To begin with, we see that the tabernacle is a shadow of Jesus. In John 1:14a, the Bible says when speaking of Jesus, "And the Word became flesh and dwelt among us." It could be read, "The Word was made flesh and tabernacled among us." Jesus was a tabernacle in which the Shekinah glory of God dwelt. As we will see throughout this book, every detail of the tabernacle speaks of the Lord Jesus Christ.

If you had seen that tabernacle from the outside, you would not have said, "My, how beautiful." When you saw the Old Testament temple that stood there on the temple mountain like a mountain of snow itself overlaid with gold, you said, "How beautiful." But when you saw the tabernacle, you didn't say, "How beautiful."

It was as plain and drab as it could possibly have been. Around the tabernacle was a plain white fence, 7½ feet tall. The outer court was nothing to write home about. It was simple and rather normal. However, when you went inside the tabernacle and saw the light streaming from the seven-pronged lampstand, you would have taken a deep breath and said, "It's beautiful."

Further, as you observed all sorts of woven work and gold and shimmering beauty and purple and scarlet and blue and white colors and needlework, you would have said, "This is one of the most beautiful sights I've ever seen."

Immediately, we catch a glimpse of our first picture of Jesus. So many people were not and are not impressed with Jesus. Do you know why? People who are not impressed with Jesus are simply seeing Him from the wrong side.

The Bible says in Isaiah 53:2, "And when we see Him, there is no beauty that we should desire Him." In other words, when you look at Him through the natural eye, people say, "Well, the peasant from Galilee." Yet, when you come in the door and see Jesus from the inside, you behold the King, and He is beautiful. It all depends. Do you know Him? Have you really seen Him?

Some people wonder why we get excited about Jesus. They don't understand why we are so enamored with Him. It's likely because they don't know Him like we do. The only way to know Jesus is for God to show Him to us by His mercy and grace.

The natural man cannot perceive Jesus with his natural senses. In 1 Corinthians 2:14, we read, "But the natural man does not receive the things of the Spirit of God, for they are foolishness to him; nor can he know them, because they are spiritually discerned."

As you read this book and learn about the tabernacle, I pray that you will see more of Jesus. If He isn't beautiful to you yet, you may need to enter in through that door and you'll see the tabernacle from the inside and not from the outside. The only way to really see the tabernacle and to see Jesus is from the inside. You must come through the door. In John 10:7, Jesus said about Himself, "I am the door."

To come *to* Jesus, you must come *through* Him.

Second Basic Truth: The Tabernacle is a Blueprint of the Believer

The second thing I want you to notice about the tabernacle is that it is a blueprint of the believer. If you recall, the tabernacle had three rooms: the outer court, the inner court, and the innermost court. These rooms picture the triune nature of man. For you see, man is a house of three rooms.

In 1 Thessalonians 5:23b, the Bible teaches, "and may your whole spirit, soul, and body be preserved blameless at the coming of our

Lord Jesus Christ." With your body, you have your physical life. With your soul you have psychological life. The Greek word for soul is the word we get the words psychology, psychiatry, and psyche from. Then with your spirit you have spiritual life. John 4:24 expresses it this way, "God is Spirit, and those who worship Him must worship in spirit and truth." All of us, as humans, have three kinds of life: physical life, psychological life, and spiritual life. Each of these aspects of our lives is pictured by the tabernacle.

What does that outer court represent? It represents the body, the part of each other that we see. When you consider the furniture in the outer court, it is all related to the body. The outer court contained the brazen altar where sacrifices were made. In Romans 12:1a, we are told, "I beseech you therefore, brethren, by the mercies of God, that you present your bodies a living sacrifice." God wants us to lay down our bodies in service to Him.

Next, in the inner court, we see the representation of the soul. This court was the place of worship and fellowship, those things needed by the inner person. The believers were able to communicate soul to soul in the inner court.

Finally, we look to the innermost court, which was also called the Holy of Holies. This was the inner sanctum, and it represents the spirit of a person. God's Shekinah glory dwelt in that back room, in that Holy of Holies. Similarly, God's Spirit dwells in the inner spirit of a man or woman who knows Him. God's Spirit bears witness with my spirit that I am a child of God (see Romans 8:16). That Holy of Holies was the place of deepest, individual, personal communion. It's where we commune with God Almighty.

In John 14:17, we read, "the Spirit of truth, whom the world cannot receive, because it neither sees Him nor knows Him; but you know Him, for He dwells with you and will be in you."

So, you see, you are a tabernacle.

Third Basic Truth: The Tabernacle is a Shadow of Salvation

The third thing we can learn from the tabernacle is that it is a shadow of salvation. In simple terms, the tabernacle tells us how we can come to God.

Let's think about the furniture that is in the tabernacle and what it pictures. As you walk through the door of the tabernacle, you would see the brazen altar. Then you would come to the laver. Walking past the laver, you would approach the table of showbread. On this table would be loaves of bread.

Next, if you turn to your left, you will see the lampstand glowing and burning. It would be made of gold, and it would have seven prongs in it. Actually, it had one main stem representing God and six branches representing man.

As you walk a little further, you would see an altar of incense, and there would be smoke going up—sweet smelling, perfumed smoke burning all the time. Continuing on, you would walk right on in to the Holy of Holies. In this innermost court, you would see two more pieces of furniture: the Ark of the Covenant and the mercy seat.

Interestingly, if you look at all of these pieces of furniture together, they form the shape of the cross. Starting at the foot of the cross, you come right on through. I don't think that's by chance or by accident, though some may. The sequence of these pieces of furniture is very logical and yet very spiritual.

How the Tabernacle Furniture Speaks of Christ and Salvation

First, the brazen altar speaks of Christ, our sacrifice, because it was there the blood was shed. The animal was offered there.

Next as you come to the laver, you are washed in this place. What does this speak of? This speaks of Christ, our sanctification. Christ is our sacrifice and our sanctification. The Bible says, in 1 John 1:7, "But if we walk in the light as He is in the light, we have fellowship with one another, and the blood of Jesus Christ His Son cleanses us from all sin." In Christ, we are cleansed by His blood and washed by the water of the Word (see Ephesians 5:26).

Moving forward, we look at the significance of the showbread table. What does this piece of furniture represent? Christ is our sustenance. Not only does He forgive us, not only does He cleanse us, but He also sustains us. And we must feed on Him. He is the bread of life.

Next, we look to the lampstand. What does it represent? Christ is our sight. He is the light of the world. In Him we find substance and sustenance, and we also find sight. It is in Christ that we can see. As the Bible teaches us in John 3:5, "unless one is born of water and the Spirit, he cannot enter the kingdom of God."

Then, we come up to the altar of incense. This incense is sending up sweet, perfumed smoke. What does this represent? Symbolically, it stands for prayer. In Revelation 5:8 we read, "Now when He had taken the scroll, the four living creatures and the twenty-four elders fell down before the Lamb, each having a harp, and golden bowls full of incense, which are the prayers of the saints." The sweet smells rising are our prayers. The Lord is teaching that just as the smoke ascended from the tabernacle up and into the nostrils of God, so also our prayers are to be like a sweet smell to Him. Our prayers are to be a savor continually rising up to God.

In addition, we learn we can pray through Jesus and in His name. The Bible teaches us that Jesus prays for us. In Hebrews 7:25, we read that Jesus, "always lives to make intercession for them." The altar of incense speaks of Christ, my supplication, the One *to* whom I pray, and the One *through* whom I pray.

Next, we come right into the Holy of Holies. This place represents Christ, our satisfaction, our all in all. When you come the way of the cross, when you start with the blood and come past the laver and feed on the bread and walk in the light and pray in the spirit, then you will know something of the communion in that innermost cube. The inner room represents Christ, our satisfaction.

Comparing the Old and New Testament Symbols

Perhaps you are wondering if I'm correct regarding meaning and symbolism. Let's look at some instances in the New Testament and compare them to these references in Exodus.

First, look at John 1:29, "The next day John saw Jesus coming toward him, and said, "Behold! The Lamb of God who takes away the sin of the world!" That is Christ, our sacrifice—the Lamb of God, the sacrificial lamb.

Now consider the words of John 3:5, "Jesus answered, 'Most assuredly, I say to you, unless one is born of water and the Spirit, he cannot enter the kingdom of God.'" What was in the laver? Water. This is not talking about baptism now. Don't mistake it. It is talking about being born again by the washing of water, by regeneration, the washing of the word of God. Christ washes us because He is our sanctification.

Continuing on, look at John 6:35 as we think about the bread. The Bible says, "And Jesus said to them, 'I am the bread of life. He who comes to Me shall never hunger, and he who believes in Me shall never thirst.'"

Then, consider John 9:6-7 and the story of the healing of the blind man. "When He [Jesus] had said these things, He spat on the ground and made clay with the saliva; and He anointed the eyes of the blind man with the clay. And He said to him, 'Go, wash in the pool of Siloam' (which is translated, Sent). So he went and washed, and came back seeing."

Jesus tells us He is the light of the world. John 9:39 reads, "And Jesus said, 'For judgment I have come into this world, that those who do not see may see, and that those who see may be made blind.'" Jesus is our sight. He is our golden lampstand.

Moving to the altar of incense, we discover a New Testament reference in John 14:13-14, "And whatever you ask in My name, that I will do, that the Father may be glorified in the Son. If you ask anything in My name, I will do it." Christ is our supplication. He is our altar of incense.

When you come to the Lord to pray, friend, do not come to God and offer Him little. Don't be trite or flippant. Instead, come with both hands full of the incense of His dear name and offer that to God. Christ is our supplication. He promises, "If you ask anything in My name, I will do it."

Next, we get to the mercy seat of God. In John 17:20-23, we read this heart-felt prayer of Jesus for believers:

> "I do not pray for these alone, but also for those who will believe in Me through their word; that they all may be one, as You, Father, are in Me, and I in You; that they also may be one in Us, that the world may believe that You sent Me. And the glory which You gave Me I have given them, that they may be one just as We are one: I in them, and You in Me; that they may be made perfect in one, and that the world may know that You have sent Me, and have loved them as You have loved Me."

Have you ever thought about how much God loves you? These verses in John teach us that He loves us as much as He loves His dear Son, the Lord Jesus. Standing here in the Holy of Holies, we think about our Savior, Jesus Christ. He is our satisfaction. We are in Christ, and Christ is in us. Christ is in God, and God is in Christ. Together, we are at the mercy seat worshipping and communicating in the sweetest way we could possibly know.

Closing Thoughts About the Tabernacle Overview

Do you think it just happened by chance that we walk through the tabernacle and walk through the Gospel of John the same way? Do you think these events just came by chance, beginning with the altar and going to the water, the bread, the light, the prayer, and then going on into the Holy of Holies? Absolutely not! No man could have written a book like the Gospel of John apart from the inspiration of the Holy Spirit.

Let's pray together as we close this chapter:

Father, we pray that You would continually speak to us and help us to realize that when Jesus died, the veil was torn so that we might enter into the Holy of Holies and dwell in the Shekinah glory. Father, we pray that if there are those who have seen the tabernacle from the outside, but have never seen it from the inside, that they might see the King in His beauty. For we pray in Jesus' name. Amen.

CHAPTER TWO

Christ: The Beauty of the Tabernacle

The only way to know the beauty of the tabernacle is to come in through the door and trust Christ, of whom the tabernacle speaks.
—Adrian Rogers

I n Chapter One, we set the stage for our study of the tabernacle. Let's take a closer look now at the major structure of the tabernacle. It was a tent-like structure that formed a curtained wall all around the worship area. This structure measured 75 feet by 150 feet. It formed a large rectangular area.

To launch into this part of the study of the tabernacle, let's look at several scriptures. First, look at Exodus 26:19, where I want you to notice now the foundation of the tabernacle building itself—the silver foundation or the base of the tabernacle. "You shall make forty sockets of silver under the twenty boards: two sockets under each of the boards for its two tenons."

Next, let's read Exodus 38:25:

And the silver from those who were numbered of the congregation was one hundred talents and one thousand seven hundred and seventy-five shekels, according to the shekel of the sanctuary: a bekah for each man (that is, half a shekel, according to the shekel of the sanctuary), for everyone included in the numbering from twenty years old and above, for six hundred and three thousand, five hundred and fifty men. And from the hundred talents of silver were cast the sockets of the sanctuary and the bases of the veil: one hundred sockets from the hundred talents, one talent for each socket.

As we dive into these verses, we discover more about the outer court, the foundation of the tent-like structure. The foundation of this entire building called the tabernacle was made of solid silver. Amazingly, the building rests on one hundred blocks of solid silver and each block of silver weighed approximately 100 pounds. Wow!

Can you imagine lugging five tons of silver through the desert? They did it! Every time they moved, they said, "Hi-ho, silver! Here we go." Then they would pick up the heavy blocks of silver and travel to the next camping area.

Talk about an expensive building. This tabernacle was made from the finest materials. Not only was it founded on silver blocks, but it also was overlaid with gold. It's possibly the most expensive building of its size ever built. A conservative estimate for a structure like this today would make the tabernacle worth millions…maybe more.

We will talk more in detail in coming chapters about all of the elements that went together to form this incredible mobile structure. But for now, let's think a little more about this foundation of silver. Here are three things to specifically notice about the foundation.

The Source of the Silver Foundation

What was the source of the silver? When you understand where this silver came from, then you will understand something of the symbolism and the significance of it.

Let's look at what the Bible teaches about the source of the silver. In Exodus 30:11, we read:

> Then the LORD spoke to Moses, saying: "When you take the census of the children of Israel for their number, then every man shall give a ransom for himself to the LORD, when you number them, that there may be no plague among them when you number them."

God was very clear about what He said. In essence, "Now, when you go to count the soldiers, and you're going one, two, three, four, five, six, everyone that you count you take a ransom tax from him, some blood money, a ransom for his soul."

In Exodus 30:13, God instructs:

"This is what everyone among those who are numbered shall give: half a shekel according to the shekel of the sanctuary (a shekel is twenty gerahs). The half-shekel shall be an offering to the LORD. Everyone included among those who are numbered, from twenty years old and above, shall give an offering to the LORD. The rich shall not give more and the poor shall not give less..."

Let's look at verse 15 of the same chapter, "The rich shall not give more and the poor shall not give less than half a shekel, when you give an offering to the LORD, to make atonement for yourselves." The word atonement (ransom) is very important.

Where did the silver come from? Where did they get the money to build the silver foundation for the tabernacle? It was from taxes that were levied upon the people. It was not an optional thing. They didn't have a choice in this offering.

Indeed, this is not a free will offering. In fact, it is the only thing in the tabernacle that was not a free will offering. The silver that was used for the foundation was a required offering, and if it was not made, there was no ransom...there was no atonement. The plague was upon them and there was sudden death as failure to make this offering. That was the source of the offering—an imposed, required tax.

Remarkably, the rest of the tabernacle was built on love offerings that came from free will. For the rest of the structure, they gave willingly from their hearts. However, the silver foundation was a required gift from everyone.

The Symbolism of the Silver Foundation

What does the silver foundation symbolize? It symbolizes the atonement for our souls, the atoning blood of Jesus Christ. In 1 Peter 1:18-19, we read, "knowing that you were not redeemed with corruptible things, like silver or gold, from your aimless conduct received by tradition from your fathers, but with the precious blood of Christ, as of a lamb without blemish and without spot."

Peter is making a contrast between the precious blood of the Lord Jesus Christ and the silver that symbolized that blood. We could also make this contrast: we're not redeemed with the blood of bulls and goats, but the blood of bulls and goats in Old Testament sacrifices symbolized the blood of Jesus that did redeem. Back to the silver and gold, we're not redeemed with those elements, but the silver and the gold symbolizes the silver of Jesus' tears and the gold of His blood that does redeem.

And so, what is the symbol of the silver foundation? It is atonement and redemption. Exodus 30:15 teaches us, "The rich shall not give more and the poor shall not give less than half a shekel, when you give an offering to the LORD, to make atonement for yourselves."

The Significance of the Silver Foundation:

Overall

What is the significance of it all? The entire tabernacle building rested upon the foundation of redemption. The entire building was built upon the foundation of atonement. Most tents would rest upon the desert sand. But Jesus taught us how foolish it was to build our houses upon sand. Matthew 7:26-27 says, "But everyone who hears these sayings of Mine, and does not do them, will be like a foolish man who built his house on the sand: and the rain descended, the floods came, and the winds blew and beat on that house; and it fell. And great was its fall."

So much religion in America today is like that—built upon the sand—not built upon atonement and redemption. Why is this? Because many in America have religion without the blood of Jesus. They have bloodless religion. They are building their houses of worship on the sand, not on the Savior. "For no other foundation can anyone lay than that which is laid, which is Jesus Christ" (1 Corinthians 3:11). This is the reason the silver, a very precious metal, symbolizes the blood of Jesus, which is exceedingly precious. The Bible clearly says, "Without shedding of blood there is no remission" (Hebrews 9:22b).

Some fail to understand just what the blood of Jesus Christ stands for. Do you know why Peter called it the precious blood? Let's look at a fact so many people have never understood. Look at Acts 20:28, "Therefore take heed to yourselves and to all the flock, among which the Holy Spirit has made you overseers, to shepherd the church of God which He purchased with His own blood."

In this verse Peter teaches us we are to take care of the Church of God, "...which He purchased with His own blood." Whose blood was spilled on the cross? Let me choose another word because spilled sounds like an accident. Whose blood was *poured* out on the cross? Whose blood was *shed* on the cross? Whose blood was *given* on the cross? Friend, it was the precious blood of God. "…the church of God which He purchased with His own blood."

You see, the bloodline is given by the father. The blood type is determined by the father, not by the mother. There is not one drop of that mother's blood that flows through the baby's body when that baby is carried in its mother's womb. Isn't that amazing?

If Jesus Christ was sired by the Holy Spirit, God was His Father, then the bloodline was determined by the Father. The blood that was given as a ransom on Calvary was precious blood, for it was the blood of God! That's what the Bible says, "…the church of God which He purchased with His own blood." And that's the reason Peter calls it the precious blood.

I love the words of the old hymn, "The Solid Rock,"

My hope is built on nothing less
Than Jesus' blood and righteousness;
I dare not trust the sweetest frame,
But wholly lean on Jesus' name.
—Edward Mote

The tabernacle was built upon silver. The silver was atonement money; it was ransom money. It speaks of the silver of the precious blood of Jesus Christ.

The Wood Boards

Next, let's look at the boards that are part of the foundation building. Look at Exodus 26:15-30 and let's read more about this foundation:

"And for the tabernacle you shall make the boards of acacia wood, standing upright. Ten cubits shall be the length of a board, and a cubit and a half shall be the width of each board. Two tenons shall be in each board for binding one to another. Thus you shall make for all the boards of the tabernacle. And you shall make the boards for the tabernacle, twenty boards for the south side. You shall make forty sockets of silver under the twenty boards: two sockets under each of the boards for its two tenons. And for the second side of the tabernacle, the north side, there shall be twenty boards and their forty sockets of silver: two sockets under each of the boards. For the far side of the tabernacle, westward, you shall make six boards. And you shall also make two boards for the two back corners of the tabernacle. They shall be coupled together at the bottom and they shall be coupled together at the top by one ring. Thus it shall be for both of them. They shall be for the two corners. So there shall be eight boards with their sockets of silver—sixteen sockets—two sockets under each of the boards.

"And you shall make bars of acacia wood: five for the boards on one side of the tabernacle, five bars for the boards on the other side of the tabernacle, and five bars for the boards of the side of the tabernacle, for the far side westward. The middle bar shall pass through the midst of the boards from end to end. You shall overlay the boards with gold, make their rings of gold as holders for the bars, and overlay the bars with gold. And you shall raise up the tabernacle according to its pattern which you were shown on the mountain."

Let's look at this foundation in more detail. Along with the five-ton silver foundation, we also notice some very specific facts about the boards that the people were to use in building.

First, there is instruction about the cutting of the boards. The people were told in Exodus 26:15 that they were to make boards. How do you make boards? Well, you must cut down some trees. In the Bible, trees were used to symbolize humanity. In Psalm 1:3, we read about the righteous man, "He shall be like a tree planted by the rivers of water, that brings forth its fruit in its season, whose leaf also shall not wither; and whatever he does shall prosper."

As the Bible spoke of the humanity of Jesus, we read in Isaiah 53:2a, "For He shall grow up before Him as a tender plant, and as a root out of dry ground."

I believe God had the Israelites build with wood on top of the silver foundation to symbolize the human need to rest upon the silver of Christ's blood, resting upon Jesus and His atonement.

After all, we were all once trees, growing in a barren wilderness. Then the sharp axe of God's truth was laid to the root of the tree and the tree was severed, laid low, and reshaped. Indeed, this is a picture of what must happen to every person. Before any of us can be built into the house of God, we must be cut off from that old way, that old life. Truly, we must be brought low by the axe of truth.

Once the boards were cut, they were covered. Notice the next set of instructions found in Exodus 26:29a, "You shall overlay the boards with gold." As a review, you will recall that wood speaks of humanity. Gold in the Bible speaks of glory and deity. To overlay wood with gold is to overlay God's covering over our humanity. Those of us who have rested upon the finished work of Calvary, we receive the golden covering that God gives us.

In addition, the Lord Jesus Christ is also pictured by these boards. Jesus took the wood of our humanity, that we might take the gold of His glory. He clothes us with His golden righteousness when we stand upon the silver of His redemption. As we are cut off from our old lives, we then rest upon His blood atonement, the foundation of the whole process.

Let's look next at the configuration of the boards. Notice Exodus 26:19: "You shall make forty sockets of silver under the twenty boards: two sockets under each of the boards for its two tenons." Each board had two tenons or two feet, and these two feet rested upon a silver foundation.

Although the boards had been cut down, they were laid low no longer. Now, the boards are standing up. Look at Exodus 26:15, "And for the tabernacle you shall make the boards of acacia wood, standing upright." The wood is cut down at first, but now standing. What are they standing upon? They're no longer standing upon the desert floor, no longer rooted in the earth, but now they are standing upon a silver foundation covered with gold representing the stand that we have in the Lord Jesus Christ.

Notice the two tenons or two feet that are placed upon the foundation. Interestingly, when you get saved, you can't keep one foot on the desert floor and the other foot on God's salvation. Both feet are placed safely, firmly upon the Lord Jesus Christ. You can't have one foot on the sand and the other foot on the silver. You must place both feet on Jesus.

Another interesting facet of the wood to notice is that all of the boards are made of equal height. And, in Christ, we are all made equal. In Him, we all stand at the same place of significance and importance.

Now that we have noticed the cutting, the covering, and the configuration of the boards, *I'd like to also mention the connection of the boards.* Let's look at the way the boards were connected in the tabernacle foundation. In Exodus 26:26-27, "And you shall make bars of acacia wood: five for the boards on one side of the tabernacle, five bars for the boards on the other side of the tabernacle, and five bars for the boards of the side of the tabernacle, for the far side westward."

These boards are all standing up straight and tall all around on the silver foundation. Next, the builders are to begin to fasten horizontal bars to the perpendicular boards. By attaching these horizontal bars, the boards are kept standing up straight side by side. Similarly, as believers, when we are born again, we are cut off from the old life. As we rest upon redemption, we are covered with God's glory. In Christ, we are made new. And, like these boards standing tall on an equal foundation, we need unifying bars to hold us up, keep us tied together, and keep us straight.

What are these five unifying bars? What are these things that hold us up, keep us straight, and keep us unified?

Five Unifying Bars that We Have in Christ

To understand the five unifying bars we have in Christ, let's look to Ephesians 2:21-22. God speaks of a building, and He says, "in whom the whole building, being fitted together [fitly framed], grows into a holy temple in the Lord, in whom you also are being built together for a dwelling place of God in the Spirit."

God designed us to be fitted together, just like those boards. We are all to fit together, side by side. When we're all together, all fitly framed, then we make a habitation for God. That is what the tabernacle was. It was a dwelling place for God. That's what the Church is to be, a place where God dwells. First Corinthians 3:16 says, "Do you not know that you are the temple of God and that the Spirit of God dwells in you?"

Now, I believe that's what this Old Testament tabernacle pictured. It's exactly what Paul is talking to the Ephesians about—these boards standing side by side, all of them of equal height, because we're all one in the Lord Jesus.

So, what do the five bars stand for?

Let's look to Ephesians 4:11-14a to begin to answer this question:

And He Himself gave some to be apostles, some prophets, some evangelists, and some pastors and teachers, for the equipping of the saints for the work of ministry, for the edifying [that means the building] of the body of Christ, till we all come to the unity of the faith and of the knowledge of the Son of God, to a perfect man, to the measure of the stature of the fullness of Christ; that we should no longer be children, tossed to and fro and carried about with every wind of doctrine.

What would have happened to this tabernacle when a desert storm came up if these crossbars had not been there? The tabernacle would have been blown down and the wood would have gone sailing away. But God gave five bars to strengthen the boards. I believe these are God's chosen ministries to the church.

Paul mentions them here in Ephesians 4:11: "And He Himself gave some to be apostles, some prophets, some evangelists, and some pastors and teachers, for the equipping of the saints for the work of ministry, for the edifying of the body of Christ." What are they? 1) Apostles. 2) Prophets. 3) Evangelists. 4) Pastors. 5) Teachers.

God has given these leaders to the Church, these God-called servants, and gifted men, that they might be a unifying force. You see, the Bible doesn't teach a "Lone Ranger" Christianity. There are some people who choose to say "yes" to Jesus but "no" to the Church.

Let me tell you something. When you know the Jesus of the Bible, and when you're standing upon the silver of His redemption, and when you're covered with the gold of His glory, you are also going to be united in fellowship under authority.

God has given five bars to hold His church together that we be not blown about by every wind of doctrine. This tabernacle building is not to blow down, but if you take away the five bars, it will scatter. The Church and believers need the five horizontal bars to hold everything together.

The Significance of the Tabernacle Covering

All of the Colors

Let's look at a few more symbols and truths so that we will be able to make greater applications in future chapters. We are getting to the really good part, so let's press ahead through a few additional details of the tabernacle.

Once again, go back to Exodus 26:1. The Bible says, "Moreover you shall make the tabernacle with ten curtains of fine woven linen and blue, purple, and scarlet thread; with artistic designs of cherubim you shall weave them."

We are now looking at the inside of the tabernacle. All of this decoration pictures Christ in all of His beauty—the colors, the royalty, and the splendor.

From the outside, the tabernacle was a hideous-looking building. It wasn't beautiful at all. But on the inside, you would see exceptional beauty. Illuminated by the seven-pronged golden lampstand, you would see beautiful needlework in these exquisite colors. And each color is significant in the Bible.

First of all, there was the color of linen which is white. White, in the Bible, stands for holiness. In the Book of Revelation, the robes of the saints are made of linen. This stands for the righteousness of the saints. Also, this white color pictures the Lord Jesus Christ and it speaks of His sinlessness.

Second, we see the color blue in the tabernacle covering. What is blue? When you think of blue, you may think of the sky on an amazing clear, cloudless day. Blue speaks of Heaven. Jesus is not just sinless white, but He is heavenly blue. He is the Son of God that came down from Heaven. Jesus is the heavenly Son.

Next, we notice purple in the tabernacle coverings. Purple is the color that kings and queens wore in that day. It's the royal color, and it speaks of the kingliness of the Lord Jesus Christ. He is the great and sovereign King.

Also, we see scarlet, which is the earth color. The word "Adam" comes from a word that means red earth. In the Holy Land, you see this reddish color everywhere. Scarlet also denotes the idea of blood and blood sacrifice. The scarlet speaks of the sacrifice of the Savior.

You could think of it this way:

- White – the sinlessness of the Savior
- Blue – the sonship of the Savior
- Purple – the sovereignty of the Savior
- Scarlet – the sacrifice of the Savior

Did you know that each of the four Gospel books represent one of these four colors? Matthew pictures Jesus as the King of the Jews. Matthew is the purple Gospel. Mark pictures Jesus as the suffering servant. So, Mark is the scarlet Gospel. Then, Luke pictures Jesus as the virgin-born Son of God. Therefore, Luke is the white Gospel.

John pictures Jesus as the Lord from Heaven. And so, John is the blue Gospel.

Isn't this amazing to think about? The symbolism fits together beautifully. God, in dozens of ways, has given us portraits of the Lord Jesus Christ. In fact, Jesus is woven throughout all the Bible pages.

The Cherubims

Laid upon the tabernacle coverings were Cherubim, angelic creatures. Cherubim speak of the holiness of God. You will find mention of the Cherubim in Isaiah 6:3 where we read about them crying out, "Holy, holy, holy is the LORD of hosts." These angelic beings have outstretched wings and they cover their faces because of the holiness of Almighty God.

All of this glory described by the purple, the scarlet, the white, and the blue, along with the Cherubim, was hidden to the outsider. But it was not hidden to those who entered into the tabernacle.

What does all of this picture? Let's look at Psalm 91:1-2, "He who dwells in the secret place of the Most High shall abide under the shadow of the Almighty. I will say of the LORD, 'He is my refuge and my fortress; My God, in Him I will trust.'"

Notice Psalm 121:7-9: "A thousand may fall at your side, and ten thousand at your right hand; but it shall not come near you. Only with your eyes shall you look, and see the reward of the wicked. Because you have made the LORD, who is my refuge, even the Most High, your dwelling place."

When a person dwells within this tent, this becomes his habitation. The entire tabernacle tent is a description of deity. It all speaks of Jesus. All of the colors speak of Jesus. The entire tabernacle speaks of Jesus.

And when a person was inside the tabernacle, it pictured someone being in Christ. It pictured someone dwelling in the secret place of the Highest under the shadow of the Almighty. This covering represents Christ, perfect security, our security. We're safe when we're there— inside the tabernacle. We are safe when we are pressed in close to Jesus Christ.

Salvation is in Christ. So is security. You are not secure because you get to Heaven. The angels fell from Heaven. If you're not secure down here, you wouldn't be secure up there. Security is not in a place; it's in a person, and that person is Jesus Christ.

The Curtains of Goat Hair

Next, let's look at one more feature of the tabernacle covering in Exodus 26:7a. The Bible says, "You shall also make curtains of goats' hair, to be a tent over the tabernacle."

The first layer on the inside of the tabernacle was the linen curtain. This curtain rested on the boards. This white linen represents Christ, our security. Then, the builders were to lay a goat hair curtain over the linen. This goat hair curtain pictures Christ, our sin-bearer.

To understand the significance of the goat curtain, let's look at Leviticus 16:19-22:

> "Then he shall sprinkle some of the blood on it with his finger seven times, cleanse it, and consecrate it from the uncleanness of the children of Israel. And when he has made an end of atoning for the Holy Place, the tabernacle of meeting, and the altar, he shall bring the live goat. Aaron shall lay both his hands on the head of the live goat, confess over it all the iniquities of the children of Israel, and all their transgressions, concerning all their sins, putting them on the head of the goat, and shall send it away into the wilderness by the hand of a suitable man. The goat shall bear on itself all their iniquities to an uninhabited land; and he shall release the goat in the wilderness."

Now, what on earth is all of this speaking of? Maybe you've heard the term *scapegoat*? This particular passage is referring to the practice of using a scapegoat in Bible days. On a certain day, the priest would take two goats. The first goat would be killed, and his blood would be taken and sprinkled as an atoning sacrifice.

Then, the priest would take the other goat, lay his hands on the goat, and proclaim the goat to be the *scapegoat*. The priest would confess his sins and the sins of the people and then symbolically lay all of those sins on that goat. Of course, that goat had no idea what was going on, but laying hands and sins on an unblemished goat was part of the process of Old Testament confession and repentance. Once the confession was complete, someone would take the goat way out into the uninhabited wilderness and let him go. Scapegoats were never seen again by the people.

What does all of this picture? It pictures Christ, who is our sin-bearer. Jesus is our scapegoat. Our sins were laid upon Him, and He bore them away into the wilderness. Psalm 103:12 reminds us, "As far as the east is from the west, so far has He removed our transgressions from us."

I thank God for that. I just bless God for Christ, our sin-bearer.

Animal Coverings

Finally, let's look at the remainder of the coverings that were part of the inside of the tabernacle. There are four of these coverings. Let's notice Exodus 26:14 once again: "You shall also make a covering of ram skins dyed red for the tent, and a covering of badger skins above that."

We've mentioned the linen and the goat skin coverings. In addition, there were also ram skin coverings. Ram skins are not normally red, but in Scripture it is dyed red to picture the blood atonement. You see, not only is Christ our sin-bearer, but Christ is our substitute. Christ is our security, our sin-bearer, and our substitute. This ram pictures the sacrificial, atoning blood of the Lord Jesus Christ.

Remember we read, "You shall also make a covering of ram skins dyed red for the tent, and a covering of badger skins above that." From the outside of the tabernacle, you would never see the ram skins. You would never see the goat skins. And you would never see the linen. All you would see on the outside would be the badger skins.

Don't think of the badger described here as being like a badger we see around us today. Those were not known in the Middle East at all. This badger skin is only used one other time in the Bible at which point it describes something used to make shoes. It's a very durable, rough-looking skin, and it goes on the outside of the tabernacle.

Incidentally, if you had walked up to the tabernacle and seen it from the outside, you would only see those ugly, tough badger skins. In similar fashion, when you see Jesus from the outside, there is no beauty that we should desire Him (see Isaiah 53:2). You must come through the door to see His beauty.

That badger skin was tough and protected the outside of the tabernacle. It took the storms, the abuse, and the howling desert winds. The badger skins represent Jesus. He was the suffering servant who took the storms, the abuse, and the howling desert winds for us.

We can be encouraged today that our Jesus is amazing! Just think about Him for a moment. He is Christ, our security. He is Christ, our sin-bearer. He is Christ, our substitution. He Christ, the suffering servant.

He is the white Christ of purity. He is the purple Christ of royalty. He is the blue Christ of divinity. He is the red Christ of Calvary. And all of these coverings represent Jesus who tabernacled among us.

Remember, friend, the only way to know the beauty of the tabernacle is to come in through the door and trust Christ, of whom the tabernacle speaks.

Let's pray together as we close this chapter:

Thank You, Jesus, for being everything to us and for us. You are beautiful. May those who know You draw in even closer and come to know You more. And may those who are still considering come to You, come on inside the tent, and behold Your beauty. In Jesus' name. Amen.

CHAPTER THREE

The Brazen Altar: Divine Grace

We enter into fellowship with God by the way of the cross. There's no other way but this.
—Adrian Rogers

A s we begin this chapter, let's read several verses from Exodus 27. "You shall make an altar of acacia wood, five cubits long and five cubits wide—the altar shall be square—and its height shall be three cubits. You shall make its horns on its four corners; its horns shall be of one piece with it. And you shall overlay it with bronze. Also you shall make its pans to receive its ashes, and its shovels and its basins and its forks and its firepans; you shall make all its utensils of bronze. You shall make a grate for it, a network of bronze; and on the network you shall make four bronze rings at its four corners. You shall put it under the rim of the altar beneath, that the network may be midway up the altar. And you shall make poles for the altar, poles of acacia wood, and overlay them with bronze. The poles shall be put in the rings, and the poles shall be on the two sides of the altar to bear it. You shall make it hollow with boards; as it was shown you on the mountain, so shall they make it" (vv. 1-8).

Over the next several chapters, we will take a closer look at the furniture that was placed in the tabernacle. As we mentioned earlier, there are seven pieces of furniture in the tabernacle. Each of these pieces of furniture carries great significance.

The first piece of furniture we will study is the brazen altar. It is also called the brass altar and the bronze altar. This altar symbolizes the cross of Jesus Christ. It illustrates, prophesies, and typifies Calvary and the shed blood of our Lord Jesus Christ.

Above all, I want to tell you again that all of the Bible is about Jesus. If you read the Bible and you don't find Jesus standing somewhere in the shadows, you'd better go back and re-read your Bible. Indeed, Jesus is the hero of the Bible. The Old Testament tells us someone is coming. In the epistles and in Revelation, we are told that someone is coming again. That someone is Jesus Christ, the King of kings and Lord of lords.

When we read about Jesus on the Emmaus Road after His resurrection, we find Him holding a Bible conference with those two bewildered disciples (see Luke 24:13-32). Truly, I would have loved to have been there and to have heard what He told them and showed them concerning all of the Scriptures about Himself.

You see, Jesus is in all the Scriptures. And this altar is a picture of our dear, suffering Savior who died for us.

Notice the Pattern of the Altar

To begin with, let's look at the pattern of the altar. Notice the instructions given in Exodus 27:1, "You shall make an altar of acacia wood, five cubits long and five cubits wide—the altar shall be square—and its height shall be three cubits."

It was five cubits by five cubits by three cubits. As you may recall, these numbers have significant meanings. Five is the number of graces. Three is the number of deities. We worship a triune God—Three in One.

Why is this altar five cubits by five cubits by three cubits? What does it tell us? The altar symbolizes divine grace—the amazing grace of God.

Next, we notice the wood on the altar was overlaid with brass. In Exodus 27:1, the Bible mentions, "an altar of acacia wood" and then it says in verse 2, "you shall overlay it with bronze." When the Bible speaks of bronze (or brass), it always speaks of judgment. Wood speaks of humanity. If you look at Psalm 1:3a, the Bible says, "He shall be like a tree planted by the rivers of waters."

Even the Lord Jesus Christ, as the Bible prophesied about Him, says in Isaiah 53:2a, "For He shall grow up before Him as a tender plant, and as a root out of dry ground." Humanity is attached to the earth. Coming up out of the earth, wood symbolizes our humanity.

So, what does it mean to overlay that wood with bronze? This pictures the judgment of man and it symbolizes the cross of Jesus Christ. It's both divine grace and divine judgment. Five cubits by five cubits by three cubits is divine grace. Wood overlaid with brass—divine judgment because mercy and judgment meet at Calvary.

This altar also had horns on it. Exodus 27:2a says, "You shall make its horns on its four corners." What do the horns stand for? A horn in the Bible is not like an animal horn, a car horn, or a musical instrument. Instead, this horn would have looked like a square piece of furniture with an animal's horn coming out of each corner.

The horns were used by these ancient people to symbolize power. In the Book of Daniel, we read that the antichrist is called, "another horn, a little one" which denotes great power (see Daniel 7:8).

Also, horns stand for kingdoms and strength and power. If you look at 1 Samuel 2:10, you'll see some of this symbolism, "The adversaries of the LORD shall be broken in pieces; from heaven He will thunder against them. The LORD will judge the ends of the earth. He will give strength to His king, and exalt the horn of His anointed."

To boil it down to simple terms, the four horns upon this altar speak of the power of the cross. In Revelation 5:6, we read, "And I looked, and behold, in the midst of the throne and of the four living creatures, and in the midst of the elders, stood a Lamb as though it had been slain, having seven horns and seven eyes, which are the seven Spirits of God sent out into all the earth."

This verse pictures Jesus with seven horns. If a horn pictures power and this Lamb has seven horns, and seven is the perfect number, then Jesus has perfect power. In Romans 1:16, Paul says, "For I am not ashamed of the gospel of Christ, for it is the power of God to salvation for everyone who believes, for the Jew first and also for the Greek."

Do you remember the words to the hymn, "Power in the Blood"?

Would you be free from the burden of sin?
There's pow'r in the blood, pow'r in the blood;
Would you o'er evil a victory win?
There's wonderful pow'r in the blood.

Refrain:
There is pow'r, pow'r, wonder-working pow'r

In the blood of the Lamb;
There is pow'r, pow'r, wonder-working pow'r
In the precious blood of the Lamb.
—Lewis E. Jones, 1899

Next, let's think about the four corners. Why four? The number four is the earth number. There are four winds of the earth. Also, the Bible speaks of the four corners of the earth (see Isaiah 11:12). When the Bible mentions these four corners, it doesn't mean that the earth is square. Instead, it refers to the four points of the compass—north, south, east, and west.

Why does God direct the people to set up four corners with four horns? This is so good! When God directed the builders to arrange the tabernacle furniture in this way, it was to share a beautiful picture of the Gospel of Jesus Christ. The Gospel is for everyone, everywhere—*red, yellow, black, and white; they are precious in His sight.* It is the universal Gospel for everyone. All people, all tribes, all creeds, all stripes—they are precious to God. All of God's creation matters to Him. Every corner of the globe is significant and important to Him. In every corner of the Earth, all we must do is believe in Him!

Notice the Position of the Altar

Now that we've seen the pattern of the altar, let's consider the position of the altar. In Exodus 29:11-12, God is talking about making an offering on this brazen altar. He says, "Then you shall kill the bull before the LORD, by the door of the tabernacle of meeting. You shall take some of the blood of the bull and put it on the horns of the altar with your finger, and pour all the blood beside the base of the altar."

When the people would enter the door to the tabernacle, the altar was right in front of them. Why is the altar at the very entryway to the tabernacle? Because you can't come in except by the blood. That is what it's all about. We enter into fellowship with God by the way of the cross. There's no other way but this...you cannot enter any further until you come to the cross through the shed blood of Jesus.

Maybe you've heard the words of this hymn, "The Way of the Cross."

I must needs go home by the way of the cross,
There's no other way but this;
I shall ne'er get sight of the Gates of Light,
If the way of the cross I miss.

Refrain:
The way of the cross leads home,
The way of the cross leads home;
It is sweet to know, as I onward go,
The way of the cross leads home.
—Jessie Pounds, 1906

Yes. You can grow in grace, pray with fervor, and serve with great energy. You can also love others wholeheartedly and give away all of your possessions. You can rejoice and worship with your heart on fire. However, the only thing worthwhile and lasting gets God's approval as you come to the altar. The altar is the only way to God.

Hebrews 9:22 reminds us, "…without shedding of blood there is no remission." In this day and age, I truly believe the devil would like to get rid of this bloody religion. Some churches have quit singing about the blood. It sounds uncouth or offends people on a Sunday morning. They don't want to sing blood songs because they feel it is a slaughterhouse religion.

When Billy Graham first started to preach, he was approached by a Cornell University professor. This professor said to him, "Young man, I enjoyed your message. You've got a lot of talent, but if you ever want to be used, you're going to have to leave out that blood stuff." Billy Graham later shared, "I purposed to preach more than ever on the blood when he told me that."

Someone once told Dwight L. Moody the same thing. They said, "Mr. Moody, if you want to get somewhere in this world, and if you want to be an acceptable clergyman, you're going to have to quit preaching on the blood." Moody said the same thing in response, "I determined to preach more than ever on the blood of Jesus Christ."

Here's the truth about God. God honors the blood. And for this reason, we need to honor the blood. The words ring true, "…without shedding of blood there is no remission" (Hebrews 9:22).

Notice the Purpose of the Altar

Now that we have looked at the pattern and the position of the altar, let's take a look at one final facet. Let's think about the purpose of the altar. Look at Exodus 29:13-14, "And you shall take all the fat that covers the entrails, the fatty lobe attached to the liver, and the two kidneys and the fat that is on them, and burn them on the altar. But the flesh of the bull, with its skin and its offal, you shall burn with fire outside the camp. It is a sin offering."

This is a sin offering. The purpose of the altar in the tabernacle was for the people to make a sin offering. We also, in today's culture, have a problem. Our problem is sin.

It would be surprising if someone stood up in the Pentagon and said, "Ladies and gentlemen, the problem in the world is sin." Also, it would be stunning if someone stood up in one of our great halls of philosophy and said, "The problem is sin." Further, it would be astonishing if someone stood up in the United Nations and said, "The problem in the world is sin."

We know it is, but we never hear it on the news, read it in the newspaper, or hear it over the radio. Instead, they will say the problem is poverty, ignorance, racism, or prejudice. But those are only symptoms of the real problem. The real problem for all of us is sin. It is my problem, and it is your problem.

Indeed, the heart of the human problem is the problem of the human heart. The human heart is desperately wicked—mine and yours. You may say, "But, I've been saved." Even after salvation, our hearts are still wicked. If you don't believe me, just take your eyes off of Jesus for a few days or weeks or months and see what happens. Friend, don't you dare trust that deceitful heart. Jeremiah 17:9 reminds us, "The heart is deceitful above all things, and desperately wicked; who can know it?"

So, what do we do? Let's look next at the fire that is upon the altar. Where does the fire come from? Notice Leviticus 9:24, "and fire came out from before the LORD and consumed the burnt offering and the fat on the altar. When all the people saw it, they shouted and fell on their faces."

Who kindled the first fire upon the altar in the tabernacle? Jehovah God. From the moment God lit the flame, it was to be an eternal flame, a perpetual flame. The people were never to let the fire go out; they were to keep it burning. It was ignited from above, the way God intended it to be.

God sent this fire. We don't know whether it was a bolt of lightning or a flame that came down. But as they finished building the tabernacle and readied the sacrifice to be burned, fire fell from Heaven and consumed the sacrifice.

What is pictured in this fire? The Bible pictures fire as the consuming wrath of God. The Bible also says that God is a consuming fire (see Hebrews 12:29) and that He's angry with the wicked every day (see Psalm 7:11). When that fire fell upon the altar, it symbolized the wrath of God as it burns against sin. That ought to frighten every one of us.

People ask me why I don't sin more than I do. Yes, I sin. However, there are several things, several cautions that keep me from sinning. These cautions keep me seeking and praying to live like I ought to live. One of these cautions is the fear of the Lord.

Are we really supposed to fear the Lord? Consider the story of Noah. The Bible says that Noah was moved with fear when he built an ark. In Hebrews 11:7, we read, "By faith Noah, being divinely warned of things not yet seen, moved with godly fear, prepared an ark for the saving of his household, by which he condemned the world and became heir of the righteousness which is according to faith."

The Bible also tells us "the fear of the LORD is the beginning of wisdom" (Proverbs 9:10). Think about this: if you have good sense, you'll be afraid of the fire. You will have a healthy respect for its strength and power. Similarly, God is a consuming fire. He is strong and powerful. When I keep this healthy respect of His power in the forefront of my mind, I live a more holy life. It's just that simple. God's wrath burns against sin.

Sometimes I hear people refer to God as the "man upstairs." I really don't like this. When I think of Jesus, I think of my best friend. There is no friend like Jesus. He is the exalted Christ, and yet He calls me friend.

Now, Jesus called us His friends, and I call Jesus my friend, but, I think most of the time we'd better be calling Him *Lord* rather than *friend*. Let Him call us *friend*; we call Him *Lord*. For example, if I were to tell you, "The President of the United States is my friend"— he's not, but what if I were to say he was? Wouldn't that make you think I was special? Or, what if I started bragging that I knew famous athletes, actors, or company presidents? Would this make you think more highly of me? You might because I'm bringing these people down to my level. But, if the president or a famous athlete were to tell you, "Adrian Rogers is my friend," you might be impressed. They would be taking me up to their level. My credibility would go way up if this were to happen!

That's what Jesus has done. He has called us *friends*. We call Him *Lord*, but He calls us His *friends*. The thrice holy God of the Universe inspires awe and we need to remember this. Even as people all around us have lost respect for God, we need to remember to fear the Lord. Don't forget the fear and respect of Almighty God.

Let me ask you: Who crucified Jesus? You may think it was the Jews, the Greeks, or the Romans. They were all part of it, as were the disciples. But the truth is God the Father crucified Jesus. When we read Isaiah 53:10, the Bible says, "Yet it pleased the LORD to bruise Him; He has put Him to grief." God the Father put Jesus to grief.

Possibly, this makes no sense to you. Why would Jesus take my sin? Why would He take my sin penalty and yours upon Himself? Because of the wrath of God toward sin. There had to be a sacrifice. If there was ever a time when God might have been lenient with sin, it was when His darling Son was upon the cross. But God was not lenient.

I cannot explain it. I cannot understand it. I cannot fathom it. I cannot, but I believe it. Truly, Jesus Christ took my sin upon that cross and the flame of God's wrath fell upon Jesus.

When the fire came from Heaven and consumed that sacrifice on the altar in the tabernacle, it was a prophecy. One day, the fires of God's wrath were going to fall upon the Lord Jesus Christ. This ought to cause us to love Jesus more.

Jesus didn't cry out "stop" when they put those nails in His hands. Jesus did not protest when they put that crown of thorns upon His brow. And Jesus did not complain when they lashed His back. In Isaiah 53:7, we read, "He was oppressed and He was afflicted, yet He opened not His mouth; He was led as a lamb to the slaughter, and as a sheep before its shearers is silent, so He opened not His mouth." They spat on Him, but He never said a word.

When God the Father withdrew, Jesus cried, "My God, My God, why have You forsaken Me?" (Matthew 27:46). Much like the words of David in Psalm 23, "Yea, though I walk through the valley of the shadow of death, I will fear no evil; for You are with me" (v. 4). Jesus also walked that lonesome valley…all by Himself, and the fires of God's wrath were burning upon Him all that time. Jesus walked the burning corridors of the damned. Jesus baptized His soul in Hell.

You may be thinking, *Pastor Rogers, if a sinner goes to Hell, doesn't he stay there for all eternity? Jesus was only there on the cross for a little bit of time. So how did He take my hell?*

The eternities were compressed upon Jesus at Calvary. Just as the sin of the world was distilled upon Him, all the suffering of all the world fell upon one man at one point. Jesus took it all. Praise His holy name.

The fire of Jehovah fell upon that altar. It was fire from Heaven. It wasn't what men did that hurt Jesus. It was what God did. Oh, what a Savior! May we love Him more!

Let's pray together as we close this chapter:

Our Father, we're grateful for the altar that speaks of divine grace. We're grateful for its dimensions. It speaks of divine power with its four horns; it depicts universal appeal with its four corners. We're grateful, Lord, for the blood of Jesus that cleanses from all sin. Father, I pray that if there are those who have not come beneath the blood of Christ by faith and received Him, that they'll do so today. Bless those who have been saved, that we might have a greater understanding of the price of our salvation. In Jesus' name. Amen.

CHAPTER FOUR

The Bronze Laver: The Washing of the Word

The laver speaks of the Word of God, the Word of God that reveals our hearts and the Word of God that judges our hearts.
—Adrian Rogers

A s we launch into this chapter, let's look at Exodus 30. Before we read the passage, let's do a quick review of what we have covered so far about the tabernacle. The tabernacle was a tent-like structure God had given to the Jews when they were on their way from Egypt to Canaan. It was both their house of worship and a picture of the Lord Jesus Christ.

The tabernacle is a prophecy, a type, a symbolism of the Lord Jesus Christ; also, of the way to be saved. It was God's object lesson, telling us even before Jesus came to this Earth, how we could be redeemed and how we could be saved.

In previous chapters, we discussed the dimensions and the structure of the tabernacle. In the last chapter, we began to look at the seven pieces of furniture placed inside the tabernacle. You will remember that each of these pieces of furniture told us something about our Lord's salvation.

We began with the brazen altar which speaks of Christ, our sacrifice. Now we are going to discuss the laver which speaks of Christ, our sanctification. Let's go to Exodus 30:17-21:

> Then the LORD spoke to Moses, saying: "You shall also make a laver of bronze, with its base also of bronze, for washing.

You shall put it between the tabernacle of meeting and the altar. And you shall put water in it, for Aaron and his sons shall wash their hands and their feet in water from it. When they go into the tabernacle of meeting, or when they come near the altar to minister, to burn an offering made by fire to the LORD, they shall wash with water, lest they die. So they shall wash their hands and their feet, lest they die. And it shall be a statute forever to them—to him and his descendants throughout their generations."

Now, the laver was a great wash basin. Verse 18 says it was made of bronze. When we see anything about bronze in the Bible, it speaks of judgment. Brass or bronze are symbols of judgment.

Where Did They Get the Bronze?

Perhaps you read about this bronze laver and wonder where they got the bronze? The source of this metal was remarkable. If you go back to Exodus 38:8, you will read, "He made the laver of bronze and its base of bronze, from the bronze mirrors of the serving women who assembled at the door of the tabernacle of meeting."

Where did Moses get all this bronze? He got it from the ladies. And why did the ladies have all of this? Their mirrors were made of it.

Today, we are blessed to have glass mirrors, but they didn't have glass in the Bible. Instead, they had highly reflective surfaces made of high-polished bronze. I've had the chance to see these mirrors in museums that date back even before the time of Christ. When holding up one of these well-polished mirrors, you can get a clear reflection.

Old Testament women could look into one of these surfaces and see how beautiful they looked. When Moses was collecting materials for the tabernacle, the women in the crowd donated their mirrors. In order that a laver may be formed, they gave up their very own possessions. This must have been a sweet sacrifice.

So, why was this laver so important? And what does the laver symbolize in the Bible?

What Does it Symbolize?

As we consider the laver, I'm very certain that it symbolizes the Word of God. James 1:22-24 says, "But be doers of the word, and not hearers only, deceiving yourselves. For if anyone is a hearer of the word and not a doer, he is like a man observing his natural face in a mirror; for he observes himself, goes away, and immediately forgets what kind of man he was."

Clearly, James is talking about the Word of God. We are told it is like a mirror. Thus, the laver symbolizes the Word of God. The bronze on the mirror symbolizes judgment. And the mirror itself speaks of reflection and revelation.

When I open the Bible, I see myself. It tells me what I look like, and it tells me that I'm under judgment. It tells me that I'm under condemnation. The laver speaks of the Word of God that reveals and judges our hearts.

Additionally, the Word of God is like the laver because the Bible cleanses us. First, God reveals our sin, then He judges our sin, and finally He cleanses our sin.

What Was Put Within It?

Let's consider what was put inside the laver. What did the people put in the basin? To get the answer, let's go to Exodus 30:18, "You shall also make a laver of bronze, with its base also of bronze, for washing. You shall put it between the tabernacle of meeting and the altar. And you shall put water in it."

What does the water symbolize? We don't have to read into this or guess. It's very clear to anyone who understands the figures of the Bible that water is also a picture, a type of the Word of God.

Let's just thumb through some passages of Scripture and notice some references to water. In Ephesians 5:25, the Bible speaks of Christ who gave Himself for the Church. Then verse 26 tells us why, "That He might sanctify and cleanse her [the Church] with the washing of water by the word."

Do you see that? Jesus sanctifies His Church, and He cleanses His Church with water. What kind of water is it? "...the washing of water by the word." In other words, the Word of God is to my spirit what water is to my body. The Word of God cleanses.

Next, look at John 15:3 for a moment, "You are already clean because of the word which I have spoken to you." Jesus says the Word of God cleanses us just as water cleansed those priests in the Old Testament.

Then in John 17:17, the Lord Jesus Christ is praying that His disciples might be sanctified, or cleansed: "Sanctify them by Your truth. Your word is truth."

The Bible, God's Word, is like the rain that comes down from Heaven. Isaiah 55:10 puts it this way, "For as the rain comes down, and the snow from heaven, and do not return there, but water the earth, and make it bring forth and bud, that it may give seed to the sower and bread to the eater."

Paul writes that the Bible is like water that washes. Consider the words of Ephesians 5:25-26 again, "Husbands, love your wives, just as Christ also loved the church and gave Himself for her, that He might sanctify and cleanse her with the washing of water by the word."

Let's review: what does the laver stand for?

First, the bronze made from the mirrors speaks of the Word of God that reveals and judges our sin. But then, bless God, the Word of God cleanses us from our sin. If we put it altogether, this bronze laver speaks of the sanctifying power of the Word of God.

Now, the next thing I want you to notice is a further meaning of the laver. If we see that the laver speaks of the Word of God, let's see if we can delineate the meaning a little more by seeing something of the placement of the laver.

Where Was It Placed?

Where was the laver placed? We are told in Exodus 30:18b, "You shall put it between the tabernacle of meeting and the altar. And you shall put water in it." To understand the placement of the laver, imagine yourself standing in the entryway of the tabernacle. You've come to the altar. Now, immediately past the altar is the laver. Then, immediately past the laver is the holy place, the place of service.

If a priest tried to go into the place of service without washing at the laver, the result was death. First, he had to go to the altar, then the laver, and then the holy place.

So, what is the meaning? What is God telling us? God is telling us that after we have been reconciled by the blood of Jesus, we need to be sanctified by the Word of God. The altar comes first; it speaks of reconciliation. The laver comes next; it speaks of sanctification. Truly, the laver speaks of the cleansing of daily sin.

And this is just the beginning of our journey with God. Salvation is just the starting point!

I performed a wedding ceremony a while back. The very nervous groom, after it was over, said, "Preacher, is it all over?"

I said, "No, it's really just beginning."

This is true about salvation. When a person receives Christ, he has gone through the crisis that puts him in the Body of Christ, but from there on it's really just beginning!

Let's notice the method that God ordained for the priests. In Exodus 30:19-21, we read about God's instructions the priests were to follow:

> "For Aaron and his sons shall wash their hands and their feet in water from it. When they go into the tabernacle of meeting, or when they come near the altar to minister, to burn an offering made by fire to the LORD, they shall wash with water, lest they die. So they shall wash their hands and their feet, lest they die. And it shall be a statute forever to them—to him and his descendants throughout their generations."

Before the priests could minister, they had to get clean. They were told to wash before they served. They were to be clean vessels of the Lord.

Can I tell you that I always wash at the laver before I preach? Our music pastor and other pastors always wash at the laver before they attempt to serve those who come to our church. We must be clean in order to serve others.

So also must you! Before you teach, or sing, or share, or give, you must stop by the laver and wash. The laver always stands between the cross and the place of service. This is where we must go continually, hundreds and hundreds and hundreds and hundreds of times.

Those priests, as they ministered, would stop, and wash their hands and wash their feet. The laver doubtless was the most used piece of furniture in all of the tabernacle, for it speaks of our coming to our Lord daily in His word and getting our lives cleansed and fit for service.

How Do You Spend Time at the Laver?

How do you spend time at the laver? Do you just open the Bible and jump right in? Yes. It's the laver—the precious Word of God! The reflection of it reveals our sins, the bronze of it judges our sins, and the water of it cleanses our sins.

But we're not fit for service until we come past the laver. If you're not spending time washing every day at the laver, just as those Old Testament priests had to do, then your ministry will be a ministry of death rather than a ministry of life.

You see, it's not a matter of the priest getting saved when he comes to the laver. When priests were put into the priesthood, they were brought to the door of the tabernacle. They were given a ceremonial bath. That is, they were washed all over. Look in Exodus 29:4 for a moment: "And Aaron and his sons you shall bring to the door of the tabernacle of meeting, and you shall wash them with water." This had nothing to do with the laver. They weren't washed at the laver. They were washed right there at the door and right by the altar.

This kind of washing symbolized a man getting saved and getting all of his sins forgiven, being washed from the crown of his head to the sole of his feet. That's the way the priest was washed.

Now, once a priest had this kind of bath, he never had another one of these ceremonial baths. It was a once-for-all bath that was right there at the door. But then he had to go by the laver every day and wash his hands and wash his feet before he could serve. In order for him to be a priest, he had to be bathed all over. But before he could serve, day-by-day, he had to wash at the laver. Do you get the connection? Do you see what God is saying?

When I got saved, I was bathed all over. When God saved me, I was made clean from the crown of my head to the soles of my feet. I came to Jesus, and I was born again. The Bible calls that in Titus 3:5, "the washing of regeneration." Just as those Old Testament priests were washed, I was washed. I was sanctified. I was made whole and clean.

But there was something remarkable about those Old Testament priests who had this bath all over. When they would go into the tabernacle to minister, they were walking on the ground. Did you know there was no floor in the outer court of the tabernacle? When you read the description of the tabernacle, you will notice the outer court floors were just dirt. The little building cost over 2 million dollars and it didn't even have a floor in it. The priests would have to walk across the dirt.

Additionally, there were no chairs in the tabernacle. There was no way a priest, when he was ministering, could sit down and take his feet off the ground. Constantly, his feet were walking on the dirt, on the dusty desert floor. But when he was in that tabernacle, this is symbolic of our being in Christ because the tabernacle spoke of Christ. The Bible says in John 1:14, "The Word became flesh and dwelt [tabernacled] among us." The Bible also says in 2 Corinthians 5:17, "Therefore, if anyone is in Christ [in the tabernacle], he is a new creation; old things have passed away; behold, all things have become new." Thus, we learn the priest was in the tabernacle, but he was on the ground.

Does that ring a bell with you? It is the position every one of us is in right now. We live in a very dirty world, even though we're in Christ. When we got saved, we stopped at the door by the altar and were washed from the top of our head to the soles of our feet. Yet, we still walk in a dirty world, and we must constantly come to our dear Lord and bathe at the laver. Because our hands and feet have been defiled by the things we touch, we need continual and constant cleansing.

I don't know if you've noticed this, but you can hardly go anywhere without being confronted by dirty things. When you walk into any drugstore or convenience store, there are magazine covers that confront you. You can hardly turn on the television or get onto the Internet without having some sort of filth and suggestive idea spewed out at you.

You can hardly go into an office without hearing the name of our Lord blasphemed, without having somebody make some filthy suggestion. Friend, we live in a dirty world. We may be in Christ, but we're walking on the very, very dirty surface of this old world.

Now, I'm not talking about physical dirt. The tabernacle is not a picture of physical dirt. Instead, God teaches us that once we come to Him and get washed from head to toe, we will also need to come to Him daily to wash in the laver of His word because we get defiled daily. Certainly, that's the reason our Lord, when He taught us to pray for our daily bread, taught us also to pray for daily forgiveness; we need to be cleansed daily (see Matthew 6:9-13).

We need to be sanctified every single day by the Word of God.

Why Did Jesus Wash the Disciples' Feet?

Having shared all that I have about the laver, it may make more sense now to look at why Jesus washed the disciples' feet. People have really misunderstood this thing of foot washing. But if they understood the principles of the tabernacle, they would understand some of the New Testament teachings. You cannot understand the New Testament without understanding the Old Testament, and you cannot understand the Old without understanding the New. It just works that way.

Notice the story of Jesus washing the feet of His disciples in John 13:1-10.

> Now before the Feast of the Passover, when Jesus knew that His hour had come that He should depart from this world to the Father, having loved His own who were in the world, He loved them to the end. And supper being ended, the devil having already put it into the heart of Judas Iscariot, Simon's son, to betray Him, Jesus, knowing that the Father had given all things into His hands, and that He had come from God and was going to God, rose from supper and laid aside His garments, took a towel and girded Himself. After that, He poured water into a basin and began to wash the disciples' feet, and to wipe them with the towel with which He was girded. Then He came to Simon Peter. And Peter said to Him, "Lord, are You washing my feet?" Jesus answered and said to him, "What I am doing you do not understand now, but you will know after this." Peter said to Him, "You shall never wash my feet!" Jesus answered him, "If I do not wash you, you have no part with Me." Simon Peter said to Him, "Lord, not my feet only, but also my hands and my head!" Jesus said to him, "He who is bathed needs only to wash his feet, but is completely clean…"

You see, in this day and age, they had public baths. Many places didn't have hot running water like we have today. People would go out to the public bath and bathe, and they'd come home just so sweet and clean.

But all the way home, they had to walk with their sandaled feet upon the dusty roads of those ancient cities. And so, out in front of any well-to-do home would be a laver. Before any respectable person would enter the house, he would stop and wash his feet. If there was a servant in their home, the servant would wash the feet.

In this story, Jesus took on slave labor. He became a servant. Jesus girded Himself with a towel as the most menial, lowly servants would do. Then Jesus washed their feet.

Of course, a person who had just come from the bath would not have a bath all over again, but he would wash his feet. Those of us who have been saved, we don't need to keep getting saved. Friend, that's a bath that lasts. It is once for all, just as the priest was bathed one time from head to foot as he was consecrated and set aside as a priest. But daily he had to wash his hands and his feet before he could minister because his hands and his feet were defiled.

What is Jesus teaching us in this passage? It ought to become more and more obvious to us. "Jesus said to him, 'He who is bathed [*he who is saved*] needs only to wash his feet" (v. 10). Our Lord is teaching here in John 13 just as He taught over in Exodus that once we come to God and get saved, that is once for all. He that is washed doesn't need to be washed again.

Don't miss this! Salvation is a once-for-all experience. You'll never find where anybody got saved twice in the Bible. People get saved once and that's all. But you will find that after they get saved, they must come to the laver—the washing in God's Word—so they can be cleansed as God wants them to be.

Consider the words of Psalm 119:9, "How can a young man cleanse his way? By taking heed according to Your word." When we wash in the Word of God, we are made clean.

Before we leave John 13, notice verses 12-15 with me:

> So when He had washed their feet, taken His garments, and sat down again, He said to them, "Do you know what I have done to you? You call Me Teacher and Lord, and you say well, for so I am. If I then, your Lord and Teacher, have washed your feet, you also ought to wash one another's feet. For I have given you an example, that you should do as I have done to you."

Does this mean that we need to have a foot-washing every Sunday at church? Should we wash each other's feet regularly? Honestly, there is no indication the Early Church ever did this as a regular practice. It's not an ordinance of the Church or something Jesus seemed to be inaugurating for His followers.

To catch the real meaning of this passage, you must notice what He was trying to teach His disciples. Jesus said in verse 14, "If I then, your Lord and Teacher, have washed your feet, you also ought to wash one another's feet."

What is Jesus talking about? He's saying that if He has forgiven their sins, they ought to forgive each other's sins. If their Lord and Master can stoop and wash their feet, they ought also to be able to wash each other's feet.

This is what Paul meant when he said in Ephesians 4:32: "And be kind to one another, tenderhearted, forgiving one another, even as God in Christ forgave you." If God has forgiven us, if Christ has washed our feet, then we must wash one another's feet.

So, how can you wash my feet tonight?

Have I hurt your feelings some way? Have I failed you some way? Have I done something that has offended you? Would you like to wash my feet tonight? Then forgive me, will you please.

How can I wash your feet? By forgiving you if you've hurt me or wronged me. Think about this: if my Lord is willing to wash my feet, I ought to be willing to wash your feet. Because of how good He has been to me, how can I not also show you grace?

A Few Final Thoughts

How might the laver impact your life this week?

As you prepare to teach a Bible study or a Sunday school class, don't forget to stop by the laver. If you are planning to sing in the choir or play an instrument, don't fail to stop by the laver. If you will be working with youth or children, don't fail to pause at the laver and wash. Also, if you are counseling, mentoring, or sharing the Gospel, be sure to drop by the laver.

Why? Do you know what happened if a priest went from the altar to the place of service without stopping by the laver? If he did, he would die. Literally, God would take his life. You may not physically die from serving with dirty hands and feet, but there is still a consequence. Those who minister with unclean hands and feet are ministering death. Not life, but death.

Rather than bringing people to Jesus, you'll turn people away from Jesus. Your teaching will have a deadening, a stultifying effect. Your music will not bring glory to Jesus. It may be faultless, but rather than blessing, it will curse. Your preaching may be theologically correct, but if you haven't washed at the laver, you'll minister death rather than life.

This is the laver. It's the Word of God—the washing of water by the word. "How can a young man cleanse his way? By taking heed according to Your word" (Psalm 119:9). "Sanctify them by Your truth. Your word is truth" (John 17:17). "Your word I have hidden in my heart, that I might not sin against You" (Psalm 119:11).

Let's pray together as we close this chapter:

Our Father. We want to be washed in the laver. Would You remind us each day to spend time washing in Your Word? Cleanse us and then use us. We want to serve You well and offer life to all who are around us. In Jesus' name. Amen.

CHAPTER FIVE

The Golden Lampstand: Christ, Our Sight

As we look around in our world today, we see a great need for light.
People need to see the light of Jesus Christ.
—Adrian Rogers

I n the previous chapter, we discussed the laver, the wash basin, which symbolized the written Word of God and the living Word of God, Christ, our sanctification. Because the priests washed in the laver, they were cleansed. So also washing is symbolic of sanctification; that is, being cleansed.

Let's look at the next piece of furniture in the tabernacle. You will recall, there are seven pieces of furniture in tabernacle, and each speaks of Christ and of salvation. These seven pieces of furniture are arranged in a particular order, so they represent a pathway to glory.

Now, we come to the golden lampstand which represents Christ our sight. Look at the words of Exodus 25:31-37:

> "You shall also make a lampstand of pure gold; the lampstand shall be of hammered work. Its shaft, its branches, its bowls, its ornamental knobs, and flowers shall be of one piece. And six branches shall come out of its sides: three branches of the lampstand out of one side, and three branches of the lampstand out of the other side. Three bowls shall be made like almond blossoms on one branch, with an ornamental knob and a flower, and three bowls made like almond blossoms on the other branch, with an ornamental knob

and a flower—and so for the six branches that come out of the lampstand. On the lampstand itself four bowls shall be made like almond blossoms, each with its ornamental knob and flower. And there shall be a knob under the first two branches of the same, a knob under the second two branches of the same, and a knob under the third two branches of the same, according to the six branches that extend from the lampstand. Their knobs and their branches shall be of one piece; all of it shall be one hammered piece of pure gold. You shall make seven lamps for it, and they shall arrange its lamps so that they give light in front of it.

This golden lampstand speaks in the broadest sense about Christ, our sight. It really has a three-fold message. First, the lampstand speaks about the Savior. Then, the lampstand speaks about the saints. And, finally, the lampstand speaks about the Holy Spirit.

Three wonderful, glorious truths are taught in this golden lampstand.

The Lampstand Speaks of the Savior

First, let's consider how the lampstand in the tabernacle speaks of Jesus. If you look in Exodus 25:31, you see a type, a picture, a prophecy, and an illustration of the Lord Jesus Christ, the Light of the world. Notice again in verse 31: "You shall also make a lampstand...."

Truly, there is but one purpose of a lampstand, and that is to give light. The Bible teaches very clearly *Jesus Christ is the light of the world*. In John 1:4, the Bible proclaims concerning Jesus, "In Him was life; and the life was the light of men." Later in John 9:5, Jesus said, "As long as I am in the world, I am the light of the world." Thus, it is natural for us to see this lampstand pictures the Lord Jesus Christ, the One who gives light because that is the purpose of a lampstand and that is the purpose of our Savior in this world.

If a skeptical person had looked at the construction of the tabernacle, he or she may have thought, *The architect who drew this made a terrible mistake.* He didn't put any windows in it. Well, God didn't want any windows in it. Indeed, inside the tabernacle, it was to be pitch dark and there was to be no illumination, except the illumination of the golden lampstand.

Why did God design it this way? Most of us know there are two kinds of light: natural light and supernatural light. Christ represents supernatural light. The world lives in natural light, but the Christian dwells in supernatural light. There's a vast difference in these two.

We read in 1 Corinthians 2:14, "But the natural man does not receive the things of the Spirit of God, for they are foolishness to him; nor can he know them, because they are spiritually discerned." It's true! The natural man lives in natural light and he doesn't understand the supernatural things of the Word of God.

As a matter of fact, you can listen to me teach about the tabernacle, but you'll never really understand the tabernacle by hearing someone teach about it. Instead, you have to enter into the Tabernacle (Jesus) to understand it; that is, you'll have to know the Lord Jesus Christ the tabernacle proclaims and portrays before you'll ever really understand the tabernacle. To see the supernatural light, you have to come to the inside. Those on the outside never saw the light of the golden lampstand. Those on the outside of Christ never see the true light either.

As we look around in our world today, we see a great need for light. People need to see the light of Jesus Christ. As I drive past nightclubs, liquor stores, and strip joints, I pray for the owners of the establishments and for their patrons. May they see the light. May they discover the hope that we can have in the Lord Jesus.

Do you know what our real weapon is against the darkness? It is light! You can't take a shovel and shovel darkness out of a room. You can't take a broomstick and beat it out. There is one thing darkness cannot stand, and it is light. Have you experienced that? When you turn on the light, the darkness must go. Light overcomes darkness. But, so many times, we try everything but sharing Jesus. We do everything except exalting Jesus. Friend, this world needs Jesus Christ. Your city needs Jesus. Your community needs Jesus. Your family needs Jesus. You and I need Jesus.

Anything we do that is less than proclaiming Jesus Christ is destined to fail. Darkness knows not two enemies, not three, but one. The only enemy darkness knows is light. Jesus in the only one who can do anything about the intense darkness of our world. He is our Light!

Next, we notice another truth about the lampstand and Jesus. We see that He is not only the light, but Jesus Christ is also the Lord. In Exodus 25:31, we read, "You shall also make a lampstand of pure gold;

the lampstand shall be of hammered work. Its shaft, its branches, its bowls, its ornamental knobs, and flowers shall be of one piece." It says, "shall be of hammered work." This phrase pictures Christ the Lord.

In the Bible, gold is a symbol of deity. Brass is a symbol of judgment. Now that we've come inside to look at the lampstand and the other pieces of furniture, we are no longer in the outer court. We leave the brass behind. From now on we're dealing with the gold. There was the brazen altar and the brazen laver, but now we're with the gold. The shimmering, beautiful, expensive, glorious, golden lampstand pictured the Lord Jesus Christ.

Yet we must notice—it was beaten, hammered gold. The Bible tells us that Jesus was bruised for our iniquities. Consider the words of Isaiah 53:5, "But He was wounded for our transgressions, He was bruised for our iniquities; the chastisement for our peace was upon Him, and by His stripes we are healed." The Lord Jesus Christ let the blows of this world fall upon Him so that you and I might be made like unto our dear, sweet, and precious Savior. He is Lord.

Christ is also the life. He is light, Lord, and life—all in one person. Read Exodus 25:31 once again, "Its shaft, its branches, its bowls, its ornamental knobs, and flowers shall be of one piece." What does this mean? The knobs, the bowls, and the flowers are speaking of the bud, the flower, and the fruit that grows on a branch.

The fruit is a very special kind of fruit. A couple of verses later, the Bible speaks of almonds (see vv. 33-34). Why almonds? In the Near East, they call the almond tree the wakeful tree or the tree that awakens first because it speaks of resurrection. The almond tree speaks of life. Look at Numbers 17:8, "Now it came to pass on the next day that Moses went into the tabernacle of witness, and behold, the rod of Aaron, of the house of Levi, had sprouted and put forth buds, had produced blossoms and yielded ripe almonds."

Aaron's rod was made from the almond tree. Aaron's rod—that he'd had out in the desert, that he'd used to strike at snakes with, that he'd used to herd the sheep with, that he'd leaned upon—was just a dead stick.

The people looked at it and there were leaves, buds, flowers, and fruit. This story pictures life out of death. It typifies resurrection. With the lampstand, we see the same thing. We see the bud, we see the flower, and then we see the fruit. It speaks to me of Christ, our life. It speaks of the resurrection of the Lord Jesus Christ. In Exodus 25:31, we see Jesus as light, as Lord, and as life.

The Lampstand Speaks of the Saints

Not only is there a lesson from the tabernacle concerning the Savior, there's also a lesson concerning the saint. Look at Exodus 25:32, "And six branches shall come out of its sides: three branches of the lampstand out of one side, and three branches of the lampstand out of the other side." In the Bible, the number six is the number for people—for men and women. Six branches came out of the side of the lampstand. Of the six branches, three came out of one side and three branches came out of the other side.

Let's think about the lampstand parts and what they represent. In the middle is a central shaft. Out of that central shaft come three branches on this side and three branches on that side. In the Bible, one is the number of deity or the number of unities. You may recall the words of Deuteronomy 6:4, "Hear, O Israel: the LORD our God, the LORD is one!" That central shaft on the lampstand represents the vine.

Then, coming out on either side of the central shaft are six branches making the number for men. So here God and people are in perfect union. When you put people and God together, you don't have six any longer, you have seven, and seven is the perfect number.

Years ago, as I was traveling on a boat across the Sea of Galilee with a Jewish guide, we saw a huge menorah. It was a giant bronze lampstand, a nationally known symbol in Israel. On this giant statue, there was a huge middle shaft and then six branches—three on one side and three on the other. As we passed this huge lampstand, I began to talk to my Jewish travel guide about the Lord Jesus. We spent the most delightful hours I've ever known riding across the Sea of Galilee. I described to that dear friend what I'm describing to you right now. I explained to him how this is all a picture of the Lord Jesus Christ.

As I shared with him, I quoted John 15:5, where Jesus says, "I am the vine, you are the branches. He who abides in Me, and I in him, bears much fruit; for without Me you can do nothing." In this passage, Jesus is talking about the central shaft of the lampstand, covered with buds and flowers and fruit. Jesus said as we abide in Him, our lives will become fruitful.

Have you learned to abide? Truly, it is only as these six branches would abide in that central branch that they could give light, or bear fruit. In John 8:12, Jesus said, "I am the light of the world. He who follows Me shall not walk in darkness, but have the light of life." In like manner, Jesus also told us that we are to be light. In Matthew 5:14, Jesus said, "You are the light of the world. A city that is set on a hill cannot be hidden."

How do we become the light of the world? We stay attached to Jesus, who is the light of the world. It's that simple. He is light. We are also light. Why? Because the entire lampstand was one piece of gold— one solid piece.

In John 1:4, speaking of Jesus, the Bible says, "In Him was life, and the life was the light of men." The lampstand pictures light and life at the same time. As we abide in Him and give forth light, we bear fruit. That's all. The only business you and I have in the world is to bear light and to bear fruit. We're not power generators. Instead, we just bear light. We shine it, but we don't produce it. We are not trees, just branches. We don't produce the fruit; we only bear it. To do all of this, there is only one thing we must do. We must abide in Christ.

The Christian life really isn't very complicated at all. You can reduce the Christian life to one word—abide. Just abide in Jesus. You don't have to worry about anything else. Often, I see Christians running around with religious heebie-jeebies. We are a nervous group of people. However, the Christian life is not meant to be complicated. Rather, we are encouraged to abide in Jesus, to live our lives in complete union to the Lord Jesus Christ. Then, the light, the life, the fruit—it all comes through the Lord Jesus Christ.

May you and I seek to abide in Him as we never have before. May we press in close and allow Jesus to shine brightly in and through our lives.

The Lampstand Speaks of the Holy Spirit

Not only is there a lesson from the tabernacle concerning the Savior, and not only is there a lesson concerning the saints, but there's also a lesson concerning the Spirit.

As we consider the symbolism of the lampstand, I want to point out that some translations use the word "candlestick," but there were no actual candles on the gold structure. It was a lampstand, not candles. Jewish people did not use candles, as we know them, in their worship. They never would have thought of such a thing. They used lampstands that were fed by oil, and oil is a symbol of the Holy Spirit.

Look at Exodus 27:20, "And you shall command the children of Israel that they bring you pure oil of pressed olives for the light, to cause the lamp to burn continually." The lampstand burned on pure oil. Throughout the Old Testament, pure oil was used for anointing which was symbolic of the presence of the Holy Spirit of God.

Let's notice how the oil is used for anointing. First is the example in Leviticus 8:12, "And he poured some of the anointing oil on Aaron's head and anointed him, to consecrate him." As Aaron was getting ready to become high priest, he had oil poured on his head to sanctify him. This action pictures the Holy Spirit being poured out upon Aaron, the high priest.

But it pictured more than the Holy Spirit being poured out upon Aaron; it also was a prophecy of the Holy Spirit being poured out upon the Lord Jesus Christ and upon the Church. The oil symbolizes the Holy Spirit.

As we go back and picture the lampstand, we see that central shaft in the middle which was higher than the others. Then, we see the six branches stretching out from the center. The Holy Spirit energizes both the Savior (the center shaft) and the Church (the six branches). The Holy Spirit pours power over the Savior and the Church.

Consider this truth: Jesus Christ did all that He did in the power and the anointing of the Holy Spirit. His ministry was under the anointing oil. The light Jesus gave forth was the light of the Spirit burning in Jesus' life.

This may not seem important to you. As a matter of fact, that truth may have gone right over your head, and it may seem quite bland to you that I mention this. But there is a great lesson here for us. The Holy Spirit energized Jesus for all the work He did for the Father.

Why does this matter? Because Jesus Christ is our example, and Jesus Christ is our pattern. In Acts 10:38, we read more about anointing, "How God anointed Jesus of Nazareth with the Holy Spirit and with power, who went about doing good and healing all who were oppressed by the devil, for God was with Him." God the Father anointed Jesus of Nazareth with the Holy Spirit; therefore, Jesus' ministry was in and through and by the Spirit.

Let's look at Luke 3:21-22, "When all the people were baptized, it came to pass that Jesus also was baptized; and while He prayed, the heaven was opened. And the Holy Spirit descended in bodily form like a dove upon Him, and a voice came from heaven which said, 'You are My beloved Son; in You I am well pleased.'" As He began His earthly ministry, Jesus Christ was anointed by the Spirit for power and for ministry. And so, the Spirit of the Lord came upon Jesus.

In Hebrews 1:9, we read another verse about anointing. The Bible says, "You have loved righteousness and hated lawlessness; therefore God, Your God, has anointed You with the oil of gladness more than Your companions." Jesus was highest of all, and He was anointed with the oil of gladness above His brothers. Jesus is the very pinnacle, and God has poured the holy oil out, the Holy Spirit, upon the Lord Jesus Christ. That's why Jesus was such a light throughout His life on Earth, because Jesus was burning the oil of the Holy Spirit.

Another passage that speaks of anointing is in Luke 4:1 and 14, "Then Jesus, being filled with the Holy Spirit, returned from the Jordan and was led by the Spirit into the wilderness...Then Jesus returned in the power of the Spirit to Galilee..." Jesus went to face the devil under the leadership of the Spirit. Jesus defeated the devil and came out of that temptation experience in the power of the Holy Spirit.

Notice Luke 4:18. Jesus stood in the synagogue and opened the Word of God, and this is what Jesus read, "The Spirit of the LORD is upon Me, because He has anointed Me to preach the gospel..." Not only did Jesus face the devil in the power of the Holy Spirit; Jesus preached in the power of the Holy Spirit.

And how did Jesus Christ die and then come forth out of the grave? The Bible tells us, in Hebrews 9:14, "How much more shall the blood of Christ, who through the eternal Spirit offered Himself without spot to God, cleanse your conscience from dead works to serve the living God?" Jesus died in the power of the Holy Spirit. We read in Romans 8:11-13 that Jesus Christ was raised from the dead by the Holy Spirit.

All of Jesus' ministry was in the power of the Holy Spirit. After all, Jesus is God. But when Jesus came to this Earth, He became man. And as man, Jesus received the anointing of the Holy Spirit, just like I must and just like you must. Truly, if Jesus had come to Earth and behaved as God, He couldn't be my example. If Jesus had gone into the wilderness and, as God, defeated the devil, He could never have been my example.

Although the Bible doesn't say it, I believe it is within the realm of sanctified imagination that Jesus said to Satan when He met him there in the wilderness, "Satan, I want you to know that, as God, which I am, I could obliterate you this very moment. I could defeat you as God. But I'm not going to do it, Satan. I'm going to defeat you as man."

Clearly, Jesus met Satan not as God, but as man. Jesus was man, just as much as though He were not God at all and Jesus was God as though He were not man at all. He wasn't half man and half God. He was not all God and no man…not all man and no God. He was the God man. Never has there been another like Him. He is God's only begotten Son.

However, when Jesus performed His ministry, Jesus never pulled rank on us. Jesus never did something that you and I don't have the privilege and the prerogative of doing. Jesus never said, "Well, I'm going to use my prerogatives as deity and defeat Satan." Instead, Jesus said, "I'll depend upon the same Holy Spirit power that Adrian Rogers must depend upon in Memphis, Tennessee."

You see, both the central shaft and the branches all burn from the same oil. And that oil represents the Holy Spirit. God anointed Jesus with the Holy Spirit and with power, and Jesus, through the Holy Spirit, went about doing good.

Jesus did His work in the power of the Holy Spirit. And what a wonderful, wonderful, wonderful lesson it is to me. The very same power that Jesus Christ used in His life is available to me. Furthermore, the very thing that caused Jesus to be a bright and shining light and caused Jesus to be the light of the world, causes me to be the light of the world.

The very same force that energized Jesus and gave Him life can energize me and give me life. The very same force that caused Jesus to be fruitful can cause me to be fruitful, as long as I abide in the vine and receive the oil. What a wonderful, wonderful lesson!

This is the lesson the Church learned on the Day of Pentecost when the Holy Spirit was poured out. What sat upon every man's head? There were cloven tongues of fire. Similarly, when the tabernacle was built and the lampstand was positioned, the Lord poured out the oil and lit the fire. That's what it is all about. We are to be the light of the world—those six branches united with the one central branch, making perfection.

All we have to do is abide and shine. Abide and bear fruit. Allow the lamp to burn.

Closing Thoughts About the Lampstand

I've never seen a lamp trying to burn; it just burns. I've never seen a branch trying to bear fruit, it just bears fruit when it abides in the vine. Jesus said, "He who abides in Me, and I in him, bears much fruit" (John 15:5b).

On the other hand, if the lampstand had candles on it, the candles would have burned out after a while. But the lampstand burns oil. God created us to be oil, not candles. We may not burn with as much smoke, but we will burn a lot longer as oil. The beautiful oil of the Holy Spirit will keep the flame burning.

Truly, it's wonderful being a Christian. It's amazing to abide in the Lord Jesus Christ. And it's wonderful to take the Bible and turn to something as simple as a golden lampstand. From looking at this golden lampstand, we see such an awesome picture of the Savior. Jesus is the light, the Lord, and the life. Also, in this lampstand, we see a picture of the Church—the number six, imperfect man, united with one who is sovereign, making seven which is perfection. Further, we learn from this lampstand that we ourselves give light because we are united to the same source. Our source for power and for anointing is the Holy Spirit of God.

Let's pray together as we close this chapter:

Father, we thank You for this wonderful lesson to our hearts. And we pray, Lord, You would teach us to abide in Jesus. Cause this message to etch itself into our consciousness. Seal it, Lord, to our hearts. In the name of Jesus. Amen.

CHAPTER SIX

The Table of Showbread: Christ, Our Sustenance

We need the presence of the Lord Jesus Christ with us everywhere we go.
His presence is always with us.
—Adrian Rogers

I n thinking about the tabernacle, we know it is a blueprint of every believer. The outer court represents the body, the inner court represents the soul, and that innermost place, the Holy of Holies, represents the spirit. This inner court where the Shekinah glory of God dwelt also represents the way God's Spirit bears witness with our spirit that we are children of God.

For some chapters, we have looked at various pieces of furniture in the tabernacle. The brazen altar speaks of Christ, our sacrifice, where the blood was shed. The bronze laver filled with water speaks of Christ, our sanctification, where the priest would daily wash. Next, we examined the golden lampstand which speaks of Christ, our sight; we learned that we walk in the light of His love and in the light of His revelation.

Now we come to the next piece of furniture in the tabernacle. It is the table of showbread. This table tells us that Christ is our sustenance. He is the one we feed upon. To start, let's read Exodus 25:23-30:

> "You shall also make a table of acacia wood; two cubits shall
> be its length, a cubit its width, and a cubit and a half its
> height. And you shall overlay it with pure gold, and make a
> molding of gold all around. You shall make for it a frame of a

handbreadth all around, and you shall make a gold molding for the frame all around. And you shall make for it four rings of gold, and put the rings on the four corners that are at its four legs. The rings shall be close to the frame, as holders for the poles to bear the table. And you shall make the poles of acacia wood, and overlay them with gold, that the table may be carried with them. You shall make its dishes, its pans, its pitchers, and its bowls for pouring. You shall make them of pure gold. And you shall set the showbread on the table before Me always."

Why does this table of bread matter so much? And what significance does it have? Let's look at the answers to those questions.

The Specifications

To begin with, notice the specifications of the table. In Exodus 25:23-24, we read that the table was made of wood and gold. You will recall that the wood speaks of the humanity of Christ. "For He shall grow up before Him as a tender plant, and as a root out of dry ground," (Isaiah 53:2a). In Psalm 1 we read about the way of the righteous, "He shall be like a tree planted by the rivers of water" (v. 3).

The Lord, our righteous branch, is represented in the wood that makes up this table. But we also notice it is overlaid with gold, and gold speaks of deity and royalty. Moreover, wood overlaid with gold speaks of the human-divine nature of our Redeemer. He was the God man. There has never been another like Him; He is God's only begotten Son, unique in all of creation.

In Exodus 25:24, the Bible tells us that this table had a molding about it. The KJV uses the word "crown." I think it's a good translation of the word. This crown speaks of His sovereignty, of His royalty, because our Lord is crowned with glory and with honor. Jesus is a royal Savior.

Also, we notice in Exodus 25:26-27 that the table had four rings of gold, one in each corner. Long poles, or staves, were flipped through each of the rings of gold. Why does this matter? As the Jewish people traveled through the wilderness, they carried this table. The people had to take the table with them everywhere they went.

Symbolically, we learn we also need the presence of the Lord Jesus Christ with us everywhere we go. His presence is always with us. When

I need Him, He is near. Isn't that true in your life? I know it has been in mine. He's always there to feed upon. And I thank God for His sovereignty and for His nature, but I am especially grateful to God for His nearness.

Moving on to Exodus 25:29, we read, "You shall make its dishes, its pans, its pitchers, and its bowls..." In other words, there are utensils on the table. What do these speak of? They speak of the way in which the bread was brought in and carried out each day. Additionally, these utensils tell me of the dear Holy Spirit who makes the Lord Jesus Christ real to us and available to us. The Spirit teaches us how to partake of our Lord and how to enjoy Him more. Jesus is available and near. I'm so thankful for these things.

If you look in Exodus 25:30, you find out a little bit more about the bread. The Bible says, "And you shall set the showbread on the table before Me always." This four-legged table held the bread up off the floor. It elevated the bread. Similarly, Christ is lifted up from the Earth. He is exalted and lifted high.

In the book of Exodus, there are two kinds of bread revealed. Earlier in the book, the Bible speaks of manna upon the ground. But the bread on the table in the tabernacle is not this kind of bread. It is, instead, lifted up and on the table.

Both kinds of bread spoke of the Lord Jesus Christ.

Manna came down from Heaven miraculously. Christ came down from Heaven. He's the virgin-born Son of God. Also, the manna was round which spoke of Jesus' perfection. The manna was white which spoke of His purity. The manna lay upon the ground which spoke of His humility. The manna sustained life and that spoke of His Saviorhood and His life-giving properties. And so, the manna represented Christ, the bread of life, in His humiliation.

However, the showbread represented the same Christ in His glorification...lifted up from the Earth. He is the bread upon which every believer must feed.

The Setting

Next, let's look at the setting of the table. The entire table was covered in bread. Notice again Exodus 25:30, "And you shall set the showbread on the table before Me always." I want you to notice several things about this showbread that was set upon the table.

It's interesting to note that both the table and the bread picture Jesus as the bread of life. Let's look at three verses in John 6:

- "And Jesus said to them, 'I am the bread of life. He who comes to Me shall never hunger, and he who believes in Me shall never thirst'" (v. 35);
- "I am the bread of life" (v. 48); and
- "I am the living bread which came down from heaven. If anyone eats this bread, he will live forever; and the bread that I shall give is My flesh, which I shall give for the life of the world" (v. 51).

As Jesus preached to the Jews in these verses, they could easily think back to all that was typified, prophesied, and pictured in the Old Testament tabernacle. As the Jews thought about this table of showbread, they also had to consider the claims of Christ. There are so many interesting parallels between the Old and New Testaments.

So, let's look at the preparation of the bread. To get a better picture of the bread, let's look at Leviticus 24:5-9:

"And you shall take fine flour and bake twelve cakes with it. Two-tenths of an ephah shall be in each cake. You shall set them in two rows, six in a row, on the pure gold table before the LORD. And you shall put pure frankincense on each row, that it may be on the bread for a memorial, an offering made by fire to the LORD. Every Sabbath he shall set it in order before the LORD continually, being taken from the children of Israel by an everlasting covenant. And it shall be for Aaron and his sons [*now remember that Aaron and his sons were priests*], and they shall eat it in a holy place; for it is most holy to him from the offerings of the LORD made by fire, by a perpetual statute." *(brackets added for clarity)*

Look back at verse 5, "And you shall take fine flour and bake twelve cakes with it." To make these twelve cakes, they would begin by crushing the wheat. Next, they would sift it. After that, they would mix the wheat and put it in the oven to bake. It's a great picture of the Lord Jesus Christ.

Our Lord was crushed and beaten. It pictures the Lord Jesus who said, "Most assuredly, I say to you, unless a grain of wheat falls into the ground and dies, it remains alone; but if it dies, it produces much grain"

(John 12:24). Jesus was speaking of Himself—of His death, burial, and resurrection. Jesus likened Himself unto a grain of wheat that was first crushed, for He was bruised for our iniquities. The chastisement of our peace was upon Him.

Additionally, Jesus was sifted. He said, in John 8:46, "Which of you convicts me of sin?" However, there was no impurity in Jesus. His life was very fine, very consistent. The bread for the table of showbread was baked without leaven. In the Bible, leaven always is emblematic of evil and sin. So, the bread was unleavened to represent a Savior whose body was crushed and whose life had the pressures of God upon Him but who lived without sin.

Our Savior was put in the oven and baked, for the fires of God's wrath fell upon that divine loaf so that we might feed upon it. Jesus Christ suffered the agonies of the damned for us. And Jesus Christ walked the burning ovens of Hell for us, that we might feed upon Him.

Jesus became our bread because He went through the oven of affliction. And that's what this bread pictures as it was crushed and beaten and sifted and baked, that we might feed upon it.

Also notice the portion of the bread. In Leviticus 24:6, we read, "You shall set them in two rows, six in a row, on the pure gold table before the LORD." In other words, there were twelve loaves. Why twelve loaves? Because there were twelve tribes. And who were the twelve tribes? The people of God. What is God saying in this portion of Scripture? "This bread is for my people." None of the world can feed at that table. This bread, this showbread, is for those who name the name of the Lord Jesus Christ. In addition, Israel in the Old Testament pictures and typifies the Church, which is the Israel of God. And so, this is the portion. That bread's for you, dear friend. It's for me.

Let's also look at the preciousness of the bread. Look again at Leviticus 24:7a, "And you shall put pure frankincense on each row." They sprinkled it with frankincense. Some commentators believe they kept a little bowl of frankincense sitting near each loaf of bread. Frankincense, extremely valuable, extremely precious, is a rare and a holy ointment that burned with a sweet incense. It speaks of the fragrance and the preciousness and the worth of the Lord Jesus Christ. Oh, friend, to you who believe, He is indeed precious.

Another aspect of the bread is the partakers of the bread. Look once more at Leviticus 24:8-9a, "Every Sabbath he shall set it in order before the LORD continually, being taken from the children of Israel by an everlasting covenant. And it shall be for Aaron and his sons..." Who partook of this bread? The priests. That is true, but this does not leave us out. God made us to be a royal priesthood, a kingdom of priests.

That original showbread was for Aaron and his sons. However, it represents the truth that all of us who have accepted Christ and been purchased through the precious blood, have been made priests unto God. We are a kingdom of priests.

One other interesting point to notice about the partaking of the bread is when they took it. They were to partake of it on the Sabbath. When is the Sabbath? Sunday is the first day of the week, so it is not the Sabbath. The Sabbath is Saturday. Most of us don't keep a Sabbath day, but we can keep the Sabbath every day. We can celebrate Sabbath seven days a week. Every day is a holy day. Every believer is a priest. Every place is a holy place.

When we enter into the Lord Jesus Christ, we enter into the rest that only Jesus can give. The Sabbath pictures the Christ who suffered, bled, and died in agony that we might cease from our works and rest forever in Him. He is our rest. He is our continual, perpetual Sabbath. He is the rest that remains to the children of God.

When do you feed priests? Every Sabbath day. When is that? Every day. Every day. Every day. Every day you're to feed upon this bread that was sifted and baked and that is for the people of God. You and I are to feed upon the bread.

The Satisfaction

Finally, let's notice the satisfaction of the table. Let's consider some of the ways that bread satisfies us. In the first place, bread is food to sustain us. Friend, you cannot live without food. You can't live without bread, and this bread represents Jesus. How do we "feed" on the Lord Jesus? We read the Bible.

Think back to John 6:53, where Jesus says, "...unless you eat the flesh of the Son of Man and drink His blood, you have no life in you." His flesh is bread. As a matter of fact, the early Christians were accused of cannibalism because some people didn't understand the spiritual meaning that Jesus was affixing to these words.

How do you eat His flesh and drink His blood? How do you feed upon the Lord Jesus Christ? How do you partake of the bread from the table of showbread? Jesus went on to explain this a little more clearly in John 6, "Unless you eat the flesh of the Son of Man and drink His blood, you have no life in you" (v. 53). Then Jesus said, "The words that I speak to you are spirit, and they are life" (v. 63).

What does this mean? If we are to feed upon Jesus, we feed upon His Word. Do you remember when Jesus was being tempted by Satan in the wilderness? He answered Satan in Matthew 4:4, "It is written, 'Man shall not live by bread alone, but by every word that proceeds from the mouth of God.'" Indeed, we are to live by the Bible. It is the book that is written to tell of the living Word, Jesus. You're going to be anemic unless you find sustenance and satisfaction by spending time in the Bible.

Also, we are to break bread together. In other words, we are to enjoy Jesus together with other believers. Truly, some of the sweetest times Jesus Christ ever had with His disciples were times of entertainment around a table, where He broke bread with them, and they had a whale of a good time.

Don't let the devil maneuver you away from having a good time in Jesus. It is your legacy; it is your right to have a wonderfully good time. Jesus is not a cosmic killjoy. I tell you in the Bible, when you think of breaking of bread, you think of fellowship. The Bible says in Acts 2:42a: "And they continued steadfastly in the apostles' doctrine and fellowship." Bread is not just food to sustain us; it's fellowship to entertain us.

Most of us hate to eat alone. I know I do. I would rather sit down with a friend and enjoy the food and the fellowship. That's the reason some churches call their fellowship time, "the breaking of bread."

It's one thing to be off by yourself and be feasting, but isn't it wonderful when you can feed on Jesus together and love Jesus together? In Proverbs 27:17, we read, "As iron sharpens iron, so a man sharpens the countenance of his friend."

Also, in Ecclesiastes 4:8-12 we see, "Two are better than one," and in Matthew 18:20, we read, "For where two or three are gathered together in My name, I am there in the midst of them." Honestly, I'm so grateful that food speaks not only of that which will sustain us, but it speaks of that which will entertain us.

It's also sweet to have fellowship with the Lord Jesus. In Revelation 3:20, He says, "Behold, I stand at the door and knock? If anyone hears My voice and opens the door, I will come in to him and dine with him, and he with Me." You can't have better company than that. Notice Jesus comes in as the guest because that's the only way He'll ever come in—when you invite Him in…when you open the door.

But He doesn't stay the guest very long. He becomes the host in just a few minutes. When you say, "Lord Jesus, I want You to have my all," He says, "I want you to have My all. I'll come in and dine with you, and you're going to dine with Me. When I sit at your table, you're going to sit at My table."

God sets a better table than you do, He really does. This happens when you open the door to invite the Lord Jesus in. I feel sorry for people who've never done that. They believe in Jesus, but they're not saved. Every now and then they go to the door and whisper a prayer through the keyhole and shove an offering under the door, but they've never opened the door and said, "Come on in, Lord, and let's sit down and fellowship together." He with me. Me with Him.

Bread was also given to maintain us. Consider the words of Leviticus 24:8, "Every Sabbath he shall set it in order before the LORD continually, being taken from the children of Israel by an everlasting covenant." That is, this bread was not to run out. There was to be plenty of it. The bread was to be maintained. You know, the breads of this world run out.

Do you remember the story of the prodigal son in Luke 15:11-32?

Then He said: "A certain man had two sons. And the younger of them said to his father, 'Father, give me the portion of goods that falls to me.' So he divided to them his livelihood. And not many days after, the younger son gathered all together, journeyed to a far country, and there wasted his possessions with prodigal living. But when he had spent all, there arose a severe famine in that land, and he began to be in want. Then he went and joined himself to a citizen of that country, and he sent him into his fields to feed swine. And he would gladly have filled his stomach with the pods that the swine ate, and no one gave him anything.

"But when he came to himself, he said, 'How many of my father's hired servants have bread enough and to spare, and I perish with hunger! I will arise and go to my father, and will say to him, "Father, I have sinned against heaven and before you, and I am no longer worthy to be called your son. Make me like one of your hired servants."'

"And he arose and came to his father. But then he was still a great way off, his father saw him and had compassion, and ran and fell on his neck and kissed him. And the son said to him, 'Father, I have sinned against heaven and in your sight, and am no longer worthy to be called your son.'

"But the father said to his servants, 'Bring out the best robe and put it on him, and put a ring on his hand and sandals on his feet. And bring the fatted calf here and kill it, and let us eat and be merry; for this my son was dead and is alive again; he was lost and is found.' And they began to be merry.

"Now his older son was in the field. And as he came and drew near to the house, he heard music and dancing. So he called one of the servants and asked what these things meant. And he said to him, 'Your brother has come, and because he has received him safe and sound, your father has killed the fatted calf.'

"But he was angry and would not go in. Therefore his father came out and pleaded with him. So he answered and said to his father, 'Lo, these many years I have been serving you; I never transgressed your commandment at any time; and yet you never gave me a young goat, that I might make merry with my friends. But as soon as this son of yours came, who has devoured your livelihood with harlots, you killed the fatted calf for him.'

"And he said to him, 'Son, you are always with me, and all that I have is yours. It was right that we should make merry and be glad, for your brother was dead and is alive again, and was lost and is found.'"

Let's use a little sanctified imagination. Imagine there was a pig in the hog pen who said to the prodigal, "You know, I'm tired of living in this pig pen. Where are you going?"

The prodigal said, "I'm tired of the pig pen, too. I'm going to my father's house."

The pig says, "That sounds like a pretty nice place. Explain it to me."

So, the prodigal, as best he could, told the pig what his father's house was like.

The pig said, "Well, I just believe I'm going with you." So the pig went to his father, and he said, "Father, give me the husks that belong to me. I'm going to leave home."

Now, notice this prodigal pig as he goes with the prodigal son, and they arrive at the father's house. The prodigal pig comes in and he has to eat what the prodigal son eats. You know, the prodigal son had been eating what the pig had been eating. Now, the pig starts to eat what the son eats. Why, they have the fatted calf. They have the sweet breads. They have the libations. They have all of this.

Afterwards the pig says, "You know, this doesn't taste quite like that swill we used to have. No, it doesn't have the same flavor. It has no real zing to it."

Then it's time for the pig to lie down and go to sleep. They put that prodigal pig in a nice bedroom with clean sheets. He is told, "Be careful where you walk. Don't mess up anything. Momma doesn't like you to mess things up. Don't leave tracks around the house now. This is momma's place and daddy's place. It's all clean. Here are some nice, clean sheets. But be sure you take a bath before you go to bed because you are a pig."

The pig adapts for a while but gets tired of it. Eventually, the pig says, "I don't belong here. I'm going back home. I will arise and go to my father."

And it happened, according to the true proverb, the sow that was washed returned again to the wallow. Isn't that, right?

Listen, friend, let me tell you something. Before long, your true nature is going to show up. A child of God may stray away for a while, but I want to tell you something: If he loves the Lord Jesus Christ, if he's really saved, if he's really born again, there's going to be something in him that says, "I can't stand it here. I've got to get back to my father's house. I will arise and go to my father. I'm tired of these husks."

Closing Thoughts About the Table of Showbread

Most of us have things that distract us and pull us away from Jesus. It may be something we like to watch or read that's not great for us. It could be we get obsessed with sports. Our jobs can take all of our time, attention, and interest and pull us away from the things of God. Relationships, money, vacations, popularity, and so many other things can tempt us and try to satisfy the hunger deep within. However, they are ultimately only husks of the world.

Go, instead, to your father's house where there is bread enough and to spare. His bread will maintain us and never give out. You don't have to be in the back alley eating tin cans with the devil's billy goats or be down in the far country eating husks with Satan's swine. You can sit at the table with the King of kings and feast upon Jesus.

I'd be a Christian if there were no Heaven and no Hell. He sets before me a table in the presence of my enemies. "Surely goodness and mercy shall follow me all the days of my life; and I will dwell in the house of the LORD forever" (Psalm 23:6).

Even if there were no house of the Lord, I'd be content to sit at this table, my Father's table of showbread that represents Jesus, the bread of life.

Let's pray together as we close this chapter:

Father, we pray for those who have never said an everlasting yes to Jesus, for those who have never trusted Jesus to save them. We pray, God, that this would be the day they might repent of their sin and trust in Jesus as Lord, Savior, Master, King, and Redeemer. Father, help those of us who know Him, who've been neglecting our Sabbath of rest, who've been neglecting our feeding upon Him. Help us, God, to see the preciousness of this bread and to feed upon it, that we might have life in us. Oh God, help us to love Your word, for it is Spirit and it is life. In the name of Jesus. Amen.

CHAPTER SEVEN

The Altar of Incense: Christ, Our Supplication

The Lord Jesus Christ is the One who continually and ever lives to make intercession for us.
—Adrian Rogers

We have been taking a tour of the tabernacle and taking note of the various pieces of furniture occupying this great tent. We have discussed the altar which speaks of Christ, our sacrifice. We passed the laver which speaks of Christ, our sanctification. We encountered the table of showbread which speaks of Christ, our sustenance. And we also studied the lampstand which reminds us we are to operate on the power of the Holy Spirit, who is God's heavenly oil. Furthermore, the lampstand pictures Christ, our sight.

In this chapter, we will consider the altar of incense; it speaks of Christ, our supplication. To set the stage for this particular piece of furniture, let's look at Exodus 30:1a, "You shall make an altar to burn incense on." Let's stop right here and camp on the purpose of this altar. The purpose is to burn incense.

What does incense stand for and what does incense teach? It is a type of perfume; when you burn it, it gives off a sweet-smelling odor that fills the room. In the Bible, incense illustrates and is symbolic of prayer or intercession to God.

The Purpose of the Altar

Let's consider some examples of incense burning in the Bible.

In Psalm 141:2, David said, "Let my prayer be set forth before You as incense, and the lifting up of my hands as the evening sacrifice."

The tabernacle incense burned continually as it was fed by the coals from the brazen altar. As the priest would take this mixture of spices and put it upon the altar of incense, continually the smoke was going up inside the tabernacle and perfuming the tabernacle. This speaks of the Lord Jesus Christ who ever lives to make intercession for us. This is literally the meaning; I'm not stretching the symbolism.

The Old Testament tabernacle is a picture of Jesus Christ. Sometimes people think when you study the tabernacle that you see something in one particular piece and then something else in another. We let our imaginations run wild and read things into their meaning. But that's not the case.

See another great example in Hebrews 7:25. Here we read about the unfinished work of Christ which is the altar of incense: "Therefore He is also able to save to the uttermost those who come to God through Him, since He always lives to make intercession for them." Jesus constantly and always prays for us—just as this sweet incense went up. Jesus, who is our intercession and our supplication, ever lives. Day after day after day in the heavenlies, Jesus is making intercession for us.

Next the reference to the tabernacle in Hebrews 8:1-5:

Now this is the main point of the things we are saying: We have such a High Priest, who is seated at the right hand of the throne of the Majesty in the heavens, a Minister of the sanctuary and of the true tabernacle which the Lord erected, and not man. For every high priest is appointed to offer both gifts and sacrifices. Therefore it is necessary that this One also have something to offer. For if He were on earth, He would not be a priest, since there are priests who offer the gifts according to the law; who serve the copy and shadow of the heavenly things, as Moses was divinely instructed when he was about to make the tabernacle. For He said, "See that you make all things according to the pattern shown you on the mountain."

There was a tabernacle in the wilderness, but that was a picture, an illustration, a prophecy of the true tabernacle. There was a priest in the wilderness, but that priest was a picture, an illustration, a prophecy of Jesus, our high priest. This Old Testament tabernacle and the Old

Testament priests were examples, and they were shadows of heavenly things.

When God came to Moses and said, "Moses, I want you to make this tabernacle." God said, "Moses, you do everything just like I tell you to do it," for it is an illustration, an example, and a shadow of a true tabernacle that is in Heaven where Jesus is the high priest. Just as these Old Testament priests offered incense that went up to God continually, Jesus is now, in that Tabernacle (Himself) in Heaven, offering incense that is going to the Father continually. What is the incense? Jesus ever lives to make intercession for us.

Next, look at Hebrews 9:24, "For Christ has not entered the holy places made with hands, which are copies of the true, but into heaven itself, now to appear in the presence of God for us." The tabernacle and the temple were made with hands and are copies of the true place. But where has Christ entered? "Into heaven itself now to appear in the presence of God for us."

Where is Jesus? He's in heaven.

What's He doing? He's carrying on the function of a priest.

How is He doing that? He is offering incense.

What is that incense? It is Intercession.

Friend, Jesus ever lives to make intercession for us. And so, when an Old Testament priest offered intercession upon the golden altar, it was a picture of Jesus, our great high priest, who offers intercession for us. Isn't it great to know Jesus is praying for us? Isn't that wonderful?

This is the reason we have eternal security. Let's look again at Hebrews 7:25, "Therefore He is also able to save to the uttermost those who come to God through Him, since He always lives to make intercession for them." What does it mean that God is "able to save to the uttermost?" Does that mean He's able to save the worst sinner? He is, but that isn't what this means. When the Bible says He's "able to save to the uttermost," it means He'll save you all the way. He will never let you go. Truly, He will save you to the uttermost. He will save you right down to the end. Why? Because He ever lives to make intercession for us.

I want to ask you a question: Did Jesus ever pray a prayer that wasn't answered? The answer, of course, is no. When He prayed, Jesus said, "Father, I thank You that You have heard Me" (John 11:41). Also, He prayed, "Not what I will, but what You will" (Mark 14:36). Every single time He prayed, Jesus prayed *in* the will of God. And His prayers were always answered.

What has Jesus Christ prayed for us and what is He praying for us today? Look at John 17:9, "I pray for them. I do not pray for the world but for those whom You have given Me, for they are Yours." Then notice John 17:15, "I do not pray that You should take them out of the world, but that You should keep them from the evil one." Jesus Christ is praying for us!

Of special note, Jesus didn't pray that we'd be taken to Heaven immediately when we get saved, but Jesus said, in effect, "Now Father, I'm not praying for the people of the world. I'm praying for My sheep. There's a very special prayer that I'm praying. Here's the incense I'm offering. I pray, Father, You will keep them from the evil one," from the devil.

You may be thinking how great it was that Jesus prayed for the disciples. But what about you and me? Does He pray for us? Yes. He did, and He does! Look at John 17:20, "I do not pray for these alone, but also for those who will believe in Me through their word." He might as well have said, "Not only am I praying for Peter, James, and John, but I'm praying for Adrian Rogers and John Smith and Sally Jones, and you, and you, and you, and you. I pray for all of those who believe in Me. I pray not that You'll take them out of the world, but I pray that You'll keep them from the evil one. Also I don't just pray for them; I look down through the corridor of time and I see every blood-bought child of God who will believe on Me through the ministry and the word of the Apostles. I pray, Father, that You will keep them. I thank You, Father, that You always hear me."

That's the unfinished work of Jesus. He ever lives, making intercession night and day for us, as this sweet perfume ascending up into the nostrils of God.

Not only does this golden altar of incense speak of Jesus' ministry of intercession for us, but it also speaks of Jesus' ministry of intercession through us. Jesus intercedes through us in our prayer life. The tabernacle is not only a description of deity but also a blueprint of the believer.

Look at Revelation 5:8 where the Apostle John saw a scene in Heaven that amazed him: "Now when He had taken the scroll, the four living creatures and the twenty-four elders fell down before the Lamb, each having a harp, and golden bowls full of incense, which are the prayers of the saints."

Also notice something that will get a little sweeter. Look at Revelation 8:1-3:

> When He opened the seventh seal, there was silence in heaven
> for about half an hour. And I saw the seven angels who stand

before God, and to them were given seven trumpets. Then another angel, having a golden censer, came and stood at the altar. He was given much incense, that he should offer it with the prayers of all the saints upon the golden altar which was before the throne.

This angel was Jesus and He's coming with hands full of incense. He takes that sweet incense of His worth, that sweet incense of His fragrance, and He mixes it with our prayers and offers it before the throne. Isn't that wonderful?

You see, the incense is the prayers of the saints. But then, this heavenly messenger with much incense mixes that in with our prayers. That's what this tabernacle speaks of regarding this altar of incense. It is a figure, an illustration, a pattern, a type, and a prophecy. One day, every blood-bought child of God will be able to offer his or her prayer to God not with the brass of emotions, not with the wood of human goodness, but with the sweet incense of the worth of Jesus.

With both hands full of incense, Jesus is saying, "Father, in Jesus' name, I pray." That's what this incense is. It's the name of Jesus, the person of Jesus, the work of Jesus!

Also notice, this incense was burned with fire from the brazen altar. The brazen altar represents the blood sacrifice. When you pray in the power of the blood and in the name of Jesus, your prayer is going through. Coals were taken from the brazen altar and burned upon the golden altar of incense.

You see, there were two altars. The brazen altar speaks of Christ and His humiliation. That altar is at the gate. That's Christ, our sacrifice. But the golden altar speaks of Christ and His exaltation. The brazen altar is for sinners. The golden altar is for saints. The brazen altar is for sacrifice. The golden altar is for supplication.

You can't come to the golden altar until you come past the brazen altar. Brass speaks of judgment and gold speaks of glory. Dear friend, when your sins are put under the blood, then you're ready to pray; you can come to the Father in the name of Jesus.

The Pattern of the Altar

Next, I want you to think about the pattern of the altar. Let's look and see what the altar of incense tells us about prayer and about the sweet hour of prayer. Exodus 30:1-3 states:

"You shall make an altar to burn incense on; you shall make it of acacia wood. A cubit shall be its length and a cubit its width—it shall be square—and two cubits shall be its height. Its horns shall be of one piece with it. And you shall overlay its top, its sides all around, and its horns with pure gold; and you shall make for it a molding of gold all around."

This altar of incense was the smallest piece of furniture in the tabernacle but it was also the tallest. In addition, it was made of wood and gold—crafted with wood and overlaid with pure gold. Jesus Christ is our mediator. The wood speaks of His humanity and the gold of His deity. That's the reason the Bible says in 1 Timothy 2:5: "For there is one God and one Mediator between God and men; the Man Christ Jesus." The wood and the gold of Jesus, considered together, makes Him our intercessor, makes Him our supplication, and makes Him our mediator. You see, on the one hand, He offers the wood of His humanity, and on the other hand, He offers the gold of His deity. He is both. He is the God-man.

Do you remember how Job prayed in the Book of Job? When all of his comforters were criticizing him and carping and giving advice, what did he do? Job knew that he had problems and confusion, and he knew that he needed guidance. In his pain, Job cried out, "Nor is there any mediator between us, who may lay his hand on us both."

Job said, in effect, "Look, I'm not God that I can reason with deity, and God is not man that He'll come down to my level. I'll never be able to talk with Him because He's God and I'm man. He'll never be able to understand me and commune with me because He's God and I'm man."

It's almost as though there's a dispute between a king and a beggar and you're looking for somebody to be a mediator in this argument. First, the king says, "I'll get another king to act as an arbitrator." Then, the beggar says, "No sir, you two kings get together and it wouldn't be fair to me. I'll go and get another beggar." The king answers, "No. You two beggars will take everything I have."

But what if somehow, a person can represent the qualities of beggar and king in one person? What if there is someone who can take the qualities of both, a mediator? This is what Job wanted—somebody who could lay his hand upon us both. You know who Job was crying out for, don't you? Jesus…God and man in one person!

This is what the altar of incense speaks of in wood and gold. This is the reason we are able to get through to God. This is the reason we are able to intercede because of the deity and the humanity of our Savior.

Now, let's notice the horns of this altar. Look at Exodus 30:2 once again, "...and two cubits shall be its height. Its horns shall be of one piece with it."

In the tabernacle, the Bible tells us there were four horns. The horns were on the four corners of the altar of incense. Each of the horns was covered with gold. And what does that speak of? A horn in the Bible speaks of power. Look at Luke 1:69 where it speaks of the Lord who, "has raised up a horn of salvation for us in the house of His servant David." It's a horn of salvation, a horn of deliverance, and a horn of power. The horns speak of the saving power of our Lord.

The horns in each of the four corners also tell us prayer reaches to the four corners of the Earth. Four is the earth number. Prayers and supplications should be made for all men and women. Jesus intercedes for all and we should intercede for all as well.

Next, look at Exodus 30:4, "Two gold rings you shall make for it, under the molding on both its sides. You shall place them on its two sides, and they will be holders for the poles with which to bear it." This altar of incense was to be carried. Everywhere they went, they were to carry this golden altar of incense.

What is the lesson here? Prayer is for all times and for all places. You don't have to be in a certain place to pray. Jesus is always present to hear your cry. Thus, when you go to school tomorrow, you've got to carry this golden altar with you. When you go to work today, you'd better carry this golden altar with you. When you go on a vacation, you'd better take a vacation with God and not from God because this altar is to be portable. It is to go with you everywhere you go.

The Position of the Altar

As we draw this chapter to a close, I'd like for you to notice the position of this altar. We find where it is located in Exodus 30:6-8, "And you shall put it before the veil that is before the ark of the Testimony, before the mercy seat that is over the Testimony, where I will meet with you. Aaron shall burn on it sweet incense every morning; when he tends the lamps, he shall burn incense on it. And when Aaron lights the lamps at twilight, he shall burn incense on it, a perpetual incense before the Lord throughout your generations."

Where was the golden altar of incense? This altar was right in front of the veil and the veil was right in front of the mercy seat of God, which represents the throne of God where the Shekinah glory of God dwelt. To get into the throne room, you had to go past the golden altar of incense. In other words, the way to approach God is through prayer and through intercession. In Exodus 25:22, we read, "...there will I meet with you..." Where? Right beyond the altar of incense.

The real reason that God is not real to some people is that they try to bypass the golden altar. You can't do it. If you want to come into the throne room, if you want to dwell where the Shekinah glory is, you must come past the golden altar. Have you done that? Have you come with your hands full of the worth of Jesus, full of sweet incense? Is there lifting from your life, continually and perpetually, a prayer of praise to God, for we are to pray without ceasing? Is Jesus real and personal to you? I pray that He is.

Next, let's look at how the golden altar is linked with the lampstand. Look back at Exodus 30:7-8. God is speaking, and He says, "Aaron shall burn on it sweet incense every morning; when he tends the lamps, he shall burn incense on it. And when Aaron lights the lamps at twilight, he shall burn incense on it, a perpetual incense before the Lord throughout your generations." When Aaron the high priest comes in to trim the lamps, he's to put incense upon the altar. And the trimming of the lamps and the burning of the incense and the refreshing of the incense are linked together. What does all of this symbolize for us? It tells us our intercession and our testimony must always be inseparably linked together. You can't let your light shine unless your incense burns. To shine for Jesus is to be a person of prayer. There are some people who just want to burn incense, and there are others who want to trim lamps, but the two are linked together. I don't think these two pieces of furniture were linked together by chance. I believe God told Moses exactly what to do in the tabernacle. The instructions were clear: when you trim the lamps, be sure to freshen and add the incense to the altar. These actions were to be taken at the same time—together.

In the church today, there are two dangers for believers. The first danger is that people will try to go out and be great witnesses without any prayer. But we must talk to God about others before we talk to others about God. Our witnessing attempts will fail if we trim the lamp (share Jesus) but don't remember to burn the incense (pray).

The other danger in the church today is that believers will burn lots and lots of incense. They will pray without ceasing, but they will never trim the lamp. They will never let their light shine and tell others about the Lord Jesus. They pray but they never witness about the hope they have found in Him.

When a person goes out witnessing without praying, that person is a fool. When a person prays without going, that person is a fraud. He or she is a hypocrite. When a man prays and then goes, he's a soul winner. One is not a substitute for the other. Prayer will never be a substitute for a verbal witness for Jesus, for letting your light shine.

You may be thinking, "I'm just going to intercede, just pray for them." The Bible says, "How shall they hear without a preacher?" (Romans 10:14). We are to be witnesses. The Bible says, in Psalm 107:2a, "Let the redeemed of the LORD say so."

However, God forbid that we should ever speak until we first pray.

In my own life, I've seen instances in which people will go and speak to others thoughtlessly, carelessly. Rather than bringing others to Jesus, they'll drive a wedge and run them away because they operated in the strength of the flesh. They try to let their lights shine, but they haven't burned any incense. On other occasions, I've seen people who have prayed and been filled with the Spirit and led of the Spirit and know just what to say and how to say it. When they witness, there is great power. They have the anointing of the Holy Spirit, and their witness is powerful.

The People of the Altar

Finally, I want you to notice the people of the altar of incense. Let's look at Exodus 30:9:

> "You shall not offer strange incense on it, or a burnt offering, or a grain offering; nor shall you pour a drink offering on it. And Aaron shall make atonement upon its horns once a year with the blood of the sin offering of atonement; once a year he shall make atonement upon it throughout your generations. It is most holy to the LORD."

God does not want anyone who is not qualified to mess with this altar. Notice His instructions regarding the incense in Exodus 30:32-38:

> "It shall not be poured on man's flesh; nor shall you make any other like it, according to its composition. It is holy, and it shall be holy to you. Whoever compounds any like it, or whoever puts any of it on an outsider, shall be cut off from his people. And the LORD said to Moses: 'Take sweet spices, stacte and onycha and galbanum, and pure frankincense with these sweet spices; there shall be equal amounts of each. You shall make of these an incense, a compound according to the art of the perfumer, salted, pure, and holy. And you shall beat some of it very fine, and put some of it before the Testimony in the tabernacle of meeting where I will meet with you. It shall be most holy to you.' But as for the incense which you shall make, you shall not make any for yourselves, according to its composition. It shall be to you holy for the LORD. Whoever makes any like it, to smell it, he shall be cut off from his people."

This sacred anointing oil represents the Holy Spirit and prayer. God says it's to be made with a special formula. No one should ever mix this and use it for himself or use it without proper authority. If you do, God says you will be cut off. And you could be put to death.

Look at 2 Chronicles 26:16-19 and see how God feels about all of this:

> But when he was strong his heart was lifted up, to his destruction, for he transgressed against the LORD his God by entering the temple of the LORD to burn incense on the altar of incense. So Azariah the priest went in after him, and with him were eighty priests of the LORD —valiant men. And they withstood King Uzziah, and said to him, "It is not for you, Uzziah, to burn incense to the LORD, but for the priests, the sons of Aaron, who are consecrated to burn incense. Get out of the sanctuary, for you have trespassed! You shall have no honor from the LORD God." Then Uzziah became furious; and he had a censer in his hand to burn incense. And while he was angry with the priests, leprosy

broke out on his forehead, before the priests in the house of the LORD, beside the incense altar.

What is God telling us? What is He talking about? He's telling us that these things are only for God's priests. They don't belong to other people. The truth of the matter is that Christians are priests. You may not think of yourself as a priest, but you are. The Bible says in Revelation that Jesus has made us to be kings and priests (see Revelation 1:6). We become priests through the blood of Jesus. Anyone who attempts to serve the Lord, to pray, to worship or do anything, except coming through the blood and becoming an anointed priest with the holy oil of the Holy Spirit upon him, is sure for the judgment of God.

There is no universal fatherhood of God. It's not so! Don't get the idea that anybody can just stand up and say, "Our Father in heaven, hallowed be Your name" (Matthew 6:9). It is not so because God is not the Father of everyone. Don't get the idea that just anybody can come to God and pray and get their prayers answered. They cannot! We must come God's appointed way.

Closing Thoughts About the Altar of Incense and a Final Check Up

I want you to do a check-up in your life. I'll ask a series of questions, and I want to ask you to answer each one honestly:

- Have you come past the brazen altar? Have your sins been put under the blood of Jesus? Have you been washed in the blood?

- Have you come past the laver? Do you believe the Word? That's what the laver represents. Have you been sanctified by the Word?

- Have you come past the table of showbread? Have you fed upon Jesus? Is He the one who nourishes you?

- Have you come past the golden lampstand? Are you walking in the light?

If you can answer *yes* to all of the above, then you can approach the golden altar and come into the throne room. Don't you just amble forth. Don't you just go happily tripping forward and saying, "Well, forget the blood; forget the bread; forget the Word; forget this and that." Instead, God says, "It is not for you to offer incense on this altar. Who do you think you are boldly coming into My sanctuary without blood? The only thing you'll get for your impertinence is the judgment of God."

Let me tell you something, friend. God is a holy God, and you come by blood, or you don't come at all. You come as a priest, or you don't come at all. Do not think God is honor-bound to answer the prayers of anybody who simply whistles and says, "God, come running. You're a cosmic bellhop. Here is something I want. Get it for me." God says, "You'll get judgment; that's what you'll get." But if you come past the bloody altar, if you feed on My Son, the Lord Jesus, if you'll wash in the laver of My Word, if you'll walk in the light of My testimony, then you can offer incense upon My altar. You'll be one of My priests."

Let's pray together as we close this chapter:

Father, may we come to You in the right way today. May we come to the brazen altar and be cleansed in the blood. Then, may we head to the laver, and be sanctified by the Word. Also, may we stop by the table of bread and feed upon Your Word. Remind us also to pause at the lampstand and walk in Your light. We want to come into Your presence with reverence and in prayer. We want to bring You incredible honor and glory and enjoy time with You. We love you, Lord. In the name of Jesus. Amen.

CHAPTER EIGHT

The Veil to the Holy of Holies: Jesus, Our Door

This veil is a picture of the Lord Jesus Christ. I'm not making a stretch when I share this symbolism. I can share it with you clearly, plainly, without stutter and without equivocation.
—Adrian Rogers

When I was a child, I used to enjoy the comics and puzzles in the newspapers. My favorite puzzles were those that asked you to find five pirates or maybe five animals in the picture. You had to hunt and search for a pirate's face or a kangaroo. You had to keep turning the picture and looking at it closely. Then suddenly you saw it, and you wondered why you didn't see it before. This is very much what the Old Testament is like. As we look at the Old Testament and look and look and look and continue to look, suddenly, Jesus just jumps out. Truly, Jesus is all through the Old Testament.

In previous chapters, we discussed that the Old Testament is all about Jesus. The Old Testament was the only Bible the Early Church had. When the apostles got up to preach Christ, they always took their text from the Old Testament. Personally, I love to take a text from the Old Testament or the New Testament. It doesn't make any difference to me, because anywhere in the Bible you're going to find Jesus if you interpret the Bible correctly. Standing somewhere in the shadows you'll find Jesus. He is the hero of the book.

Furthermore, the Old Testament tabernacle was a picture of Jesus. It was a house in which the Jews worshipped. You will recall that the inner sanctum of the tabernacle was the Holy of Holies or the Most Holy Place.

Standing in front of the Holy of Holies was a veil or a curtain, and that's what we're going to talk about next. Jesus, the veil of the tabernacle…the door to the inner sanctum.

Let's look at Exodus 26:31-34:

> "You shall make a veil woven of blue, purple, and scarlet thread, and fine woven linen. It shall be woven with an artistic design of cherubim. You shall hang it upon the four pillars of acacia wood overlaid with gold. Their hooks shall be gold, upon four sockets of silver. And you shall hang the veil from the clasps. Then you shall bring the ark of the Testimony in there, behind the veil. The veil shall be a divider for you between the holy place and the Most Holy. You shall put the mercy seat upon the ark of the Testimony in the Most Holy."

Thus far in our study I've given a general overview of the tabernacle in broad, sweeping terms. Then we described the furniture in the tabernacle. We talked about the seven pieces of furniture, one piece at a time. Before we move to the final piece of furniture, the Ark of the Covenant, I want to discuss the veil that divides between the golden altar of incense and the Ark of the Covenant.

The veil is a picture of the Lord Jesus Christ. For proof of this truth, look at Hebrews 10:19—"Therefore, brethren, having boldness to enter the Holiest by the blood of Jesus." The Holiest was a room that was 10 by 10 by 10 cubits. People in the Old Testament days were not bold enough to enter this room because they would be killed. Only the high priest would enter once a year with great fear and trembling. He would lift up the corner and reverently enter in with the blood. However, average Israelites did not saunter into that part of the tabernacle—ever. They were too scared to even try it.

But now the Bible says something has happened. Because of what Jesus has done, we have boldness to stride right into the Holy of Holies. Hebrews 10 goes on to say, "by a new and living way which He consecrated for us, through the veil, that is, His flesh" (Hebrews 10:20).

What does this picture? We don't have to guess about it. It pictures the body of Jesus. It pictures the incarnation of the Son of God, His flesh. The Bible clearly says that it is a picture—*His* flesh in a figure.

There are three things to notice about this veil.

The Pattern of the Veil

First of all, let's look at Exodus 26:31 regarding the pattern for the veil:

> "You shall make a veil woven of blue, purple, and scarlet thread, and fine woven linen. It shall be woven with an artistic design of cherubim."

Notice the colors of the veil. The veil was made of specific colors, and each color speaks of Christ. It was colored blue, purple, scarlet, and white. Jesus is the colorful Christ, and I want to tell you what these colors mean.

Blue speaks of Heaven. It tells us that Christ is the Son of God from Heaven. Blue to those people, even as it means to us today, is the heavenly color. When we look up on a bright day, the heavens are blue. God said about Jesus in Mark 9:7, "This is my beloved Son. Hear Him!" The color blue speaks of the Sonship of Jesus—the Son of God from Heaven. Truly, to refuse Jesus is to refuse God. To receive Jesus is to receive God. "He who has the Son has life; he who does not have the Son of God does not have life" (1 John 5:12).

Purple speaks of the sovereignty of Jesus. Purple is the royal color, the king's color. Purple speaks of the Kingship of Christ because not only is He the Son of God, He is the rightful heir of all things. He is King of kings and Lord of lords.

One of my favorite passages is 1 Timothy 6:15 which speaks of the Lord Jesus Christ as the only potentate as King of kings and Lord of lords, and it says, "...He will manifest in His own time, He who is the blessed and only Potentate, the King of kings and Lord of lords." He will manifest in His own time. You see, this is not His time now. This is the devil's time. The devil is called the god of this age. People wonder, why, if Jesus is Lord and if Jesus is King, why is the world in a mess that it's in? Because the devil's running it, that's why. Don't blame the Lord for the mess things are in right now. Jesus, when He was led off to be crucified, said, "...do not weep for Me, but weep for yourselves and for your children" (Luke 23:28). Jesus said, in other words, "This is your hour. My hour is not yet come." Aren't you glad His hour is coming? Aren't you glad He is going to have a day when He's going to show who is the King of kings and the Lord of lords?

It may seem like Jesus is getting the short end of the stick or the raw end of the deal, but He is not! Instead, He is the King of kings, and He taught us to pray for God's kingdom to come and His will to be done on Earth, as it is in Heaven, and one day it will be.

Scarlet, a dark red color, obviously speaks of the blood. Jesus suffered. He poured out His rich, royal, scarlet blood for the redemption of the world. Over and over again in the symbolism we see the scarlet. In Hebrews 9:22, we read, "without shedding of blood there is no remission" (of sin).

The last color, white, speaks of purity. If you look back to Exodus 26:31, you read, "You shall make a veil woven of blue, purple, and scarlet thread, and fine woven linen. It shall be woven with an artistic design of cherubim." All of these fabrics were linen and linen itself before it was dyed was white. What does the white speak of? It speaks of purity. Jesus is the Son of God from Heaven (blue), the sovereign Son of God (purple), the suffering sovereign Son of God (red), and the sinless Son of God (white). Look for example in Revelation 19:8, and you'll see that the symbolism is consistent all the way through the Bible. We read, "And to her it was granted to be arrayed in fine linen, clean and bright, for the fine linen is the righteous acts of the saints." The KJV says, "…fine linen, clean and white." The white linen speaks of purity, holiness, and righteousness. God has given us the colors of this veil to speak about the flesh of Christ that consecrates us and gives us boldness to enter into relationship with Himself.

Now, if Jesus Christ is the sinless, suffering, sovereign Son of God, you better be careful what you do with Him! For this reason, we can't just quickly nod, or tip our hats, to Jesus. Instead, we must make up our minds as to what we think of Him. We can crown Him or crucify Him; accept Him, reject Him. Don't try and stay neutral. You see, you've got Jesus on your hands. Jesus is one of three things—either Lord, a liar, or a lunatic. Deceiver, deceived, or deity. Make up your mind.

If He's the Lord, you'd better serve Him.

If He's a liar, you'd better forget about Him.

If He's a lunatic, you'd better pity Him.

But if you make up your mind, He is the Lord and He is deity, you can fall on your knees and your face before Him. One day, we will all have to give an account of the knowledge that God has given us concerning His Son. "This is my beloved Son. Hear Him!" (Mark 9:7).

Another thing I want to mention about the pattern of the veil is the way it was suspended on four pillars. If you look back at Exodus 26:32a, we read, "You shall hang it upon the four pillars of acacia wood overlaid with gold."

The wood speaks of humanity and the gold speaks of His deity. Also, these four pillars speak to me of the four gospels that present the Lord Jesus Christ and upon which the story and biography of Jesus hang. An interesting thing about these four pillars is this: there is no crown described for these pillars as there is for other pillars in the tabernacle. This seems to indicate He was cut off out of the land of the living. Each of the gospels tells how Jesus was cut off and crucified. By hanging the veil on the four pillars, the veil represents the four evangelists and the four gospel stories.

In addition, take note of the cherubim on the veil. In Exodus 26:31b, the Bible says, "It shall be woven with an artistic design of cherubim." What are cherubim? Cherubim are angelic creatures. What is their purpose? To guard the holiness and the sanctity of God.

The first mention of cherubim in the Bible is found in Genesis 3:24. When we think of cherubim, we often think of a little baby, a cute and cuddly cherub. However, Bible cherubim are fearsome creatures. Look at Genesis 3:24, "So He drove out the man; and He placed cherubim at the east of the garden of Eden, and a flaming sword which turned every way, to guard the way of the tree of life." Here these cherubim or cherubs are guarding the way of the tree of life. They are standing strong with flaming swords saying, "You can't come in here. Stay out or I'll run a flaming sword through you if you dare come in. You have no right, mortal man, to come in here. You have no right, sinful Adam. You have no right, carnal Eve, to come into this place. Stay out!"

The Position of the Veil

Now, I want you to notice the position of the veil. Look in Exodus 26:33: "And you shall hang the veil from the clasps. Then you shall bring the ark of the Testimony in there, behind the veil. The veil shall be a divider for you between the holy place and the Most Holy." The veil was there to divide. It was a divider between sinful man and holy God. That's the reason the cherubim are there to say to sinful man, "You can't come in here where a holy God is." You see, the veil of the tabernacle (and later the temple) was not only to permit access to the Holy of Holies; it was also to prevent access to the Holy of Holies. The veil did not say, "Come in." The veil said, emphatically, "Stay out! You don't deserve to come in here. You're not good enough to come in here. You're not worthy enough to come in here. Stay out." The veil was a clear division. For an unauthorized person to step in would have meant sudden death.

What does this veil picture for us? Jesus. It pictures the sinless, suffering, sovereign Son of God. But He is not pictured here in the Old Testament tabernacle as an invitation to come in.

I believe there are a lot of people who don't understand the bloody Gospel of Jesus. They think they are saved by emulating and following Jesus and patterning their lives after Jesus. But the life of Jesus does not say, "Come in." The life of Jesus says, "Stay out."

Jesus is not meant to be our example but our Savior. We can't match His example or ever measure up to His life. We cannot just learn about His life and live our religion trying to be like Him. You can't live as Jesus lived. You will be a miserable failure. The life of Jesus is a perfect standard that becomes a barrier to the holiness of God.

Learn this—you are not saved by learning lessons from the life of Jesus; you're saved by receiving life from the death of Jesus. When God placed this veil there, God was teaching a lesson that He has a perfect, holy standard, and man shall not come in of himself. He cannot. The veil there was a barrier.

The Jewish people didn't stand before the veil and say, "Oh, what a beautiful veil." This wasn't the way to enter in. Suppose they had brought flowers and fruits and placed it before the veil. Do you think God would have said, "Come you into the Holy of Holies?" Of course not! There was only one way past that veil, and, friend, it was with B-L-O-O-D, blood. There is only one way—the blood-sprinkled way. The Bible tells us in Hebrews 9:22, "without shedding of blood there is no remission" (of sin).

An innocent animal was slain, for God was teaching the wages of sin is death and the penalty of sin must be paid before man can come through that veil. The pattern of the veil speaks of Christ and His perfection. The placement of the veil, the position of the veil, the purpose of the veil is to say man is not worthy to enter. The symbolism is this: the perfect, sinless Son of God, by His example and by His standard, has condemned us by His perfect life.

The Parting of the Veil

Finally, let's think about the parting of the veil. For Jesus is not only the One who keeps us out, He is also the One who lets us in. It all depends upon what we do with Him. In Exodus, we find just a hint of what I'm about to give you. In the Old Testament, we learn the high priest would take blood in the basin and he would lift up the corner of the veil to go into the Holy of Holies.

But as you go over to Matthew 27:50-51, you will find yourself on holy ground. Pay close attention. The Bible speaks of Jesus who died vicariously. That means as a substitute in our place. Jesus pictured the Old Testament sacrificial animals and the brazen altar as He died upon the cross. And the Bible says, "And Jesus cried out again with a loud voice, and yielded up His spirit. Then, behold, the veil of the temple was torn in two from top to bottom; and the earth quaked, and the rocks were split."

When Jesus Christ died upon the cross—when His body was torn by those searing nails, when His body was mutilated there in the agonies of Calvary—that pictured God opening up a way into the Holy of Holies. It is only through Jesus we can come into the Holy of Holies. That's the reason the Bible says there's a way made through the veil that is His flesh. In the flesh He condemned sin, in the flesh He carried that sin to the cross, and there upon the cross He died. So if the veil is a picture of Christ, then the tearing of the veil is a picture of the death of Christ.

While the temple veil that tore when Jesus died was not the same veil that was in the tabernacle, it represents precisely the same thing because the temple was, in a sense, just a larger, permanent tabernacle. "Then, behold, the veil of the temple was torn in two from top to bottom" (Matthew 27:51a). How was the veil torn? It was torn from the top to the bottom. If a person had done it, it would have been torn from the bottom to the top. But a human could not have torn the veil. Josephus tells us this veil in the temple was as thick as a man's hand. Other scholars tell us it was about four inches thick.

One writer I read suggested that it would have been impossible to put a team of oxen on either end to have torn this veil. It was extremely thick, extremely heavy, and yet it was torn supernaturally from the top to the bottom. It was the supernatural work of God! This supernatural miracle illustrates there is now a way open into the Holy of Holies. That's what the Bible is all about, friend, telling us we don't have to come to some Old Testament priest. We don't have to come by way of some New Testament priest. We don't have to go get some bullock or goat or lamb.

Oh, glory to God, we can boldly enter into the Holy of Holies through the blood of Jesus because He died and His blood was shed. No longer does the high priest go into the Holy of Holies once a year with the blood of bulls and of goats. Jesus has opened the door for us.

Look again in Hebrews 9:23-24. There is wonderful teaching here in this verse:

> Therefore it was necessary that the copies of the things in the heavens should be purified with these, but the heavenly things themselves with better sacrifices than these. For Christ has not entered the holy places made with hands, which are copies of the true, but into heaven itself, now to appear in the presence of God for us.

Just as the high priest took that basin of blood, lifted up the corner of the veil, and went into the Holy of Holies, Jesus Christ ascended. Do you remember when He told Mary, "Do not cling to Me, for I have not yet ascended to My Father" (John 20:17)? Jesus ascended with His own precious blood and went into the Holy of Holies in glory and sprinkled His own blood there. Look at Hebrews 9:24-28:

> For Christ has not entered the holy places made with hands, which are copies of the true, but into heaven itself, now to appear in the presence of God for us; not that He should offer Himself often, as the high priest enters the Most Holy Place every year with blood of another—He then would have had to suffer often since the foundation of the world; but now, once at the end of the ages, He has appeared to put away sin by the sacrifice of Himself. And as it is appointed for men to die once, but after this the judgment, so Christ was offered once to bear the sins of many. To those who eagerly wait for Him He will appear a second time, apart from sin, for salvation.

Closing Thoughts and a Sweet Blessing

As we close out our study on the veil, I want to show you something that blessed my heart as I read the passage which speaks of Christ going into the Holy of Holies of glory and then letting His body remove the barrier. There are three appearances of the Lord Jesus Christ I want to call your attention to.

First, notice Hebrew 9:24, "For Christ has not entered the holy places made with hands, which are copies of the true, but into heaven itself, now to appear in the presence of God for us." In this first appearance, Christ is currently pleading and praying for you and me. Jesus offers His spilt blood once for all. *That is the continuing work of Jesus.* The Bible says He ever lives to make intercession for us. Isn't it great to know that I have a dear, loving Savior, who's pleading in glory for me, for you? The devil is the prosecuting attorney. But aren't you glad you have Jesus as a defense attorney? Aren't you glad that if any one sins, we have an advocate with the Father, Jesus Christ, the righteous? That's His continuing appearance in verse 24.

Second, *I want you to notice His completed appearance* in Hebrews 9:26. The Bible says, "He then would have had to suffer often since the foundation of the world; but now, once at the end of the ages, He has appeared to put away sin by the sacrifice of Himself." He did this once, not twice. This is the reason I could never let a priest tell me that he is sacrificing Jesus again. Friends, I want to tell you my blessed Savior died once for all. Believe it! He was nailed to the cross and by one offering, He has perfected it forever.

Lastly, *I want you to see His crowning appearance.* Look in Hebrews 9:28: "So Christ was offered once to bear the sins of many. To those who eagerly wait for Him He will appear a second time, apart from sin, for salvation."

Three appearances of our dear Lord. One is present. One is past. One is coming—perhaps today.

Let's pray together as we close this chapter:

Father, we thank You for Your Word, and we thank You, Lord, that all through the tabernacle You've given us beautiful pictures, glimpses of glory and portraits of deity. Lord, we're thankful that You've shown us over and over again that it's the blood of Jesus which enables us to come boldly as we do in prayer. Now, Lord, I know there are some reading that are hurting. They've just got real burdens and problems. The devil is trying to tell them God doesn't love them, and they have no right to come, and they're not good enough. But, Lord, help them to understand the veil has been torn from top to bottom, wide open, and if they'll just come through Jesus, they can come to glory, they can come to You. Lord, save the lost and bless the saved. In Jesus' name. Amen.

CHAPTER NINE

The Ark of the Covenant: Christ, Our Security

*You and I are not saved by keeping the law. Instead, we are saved
through Christ.*
—Adrian Rogers

I f you've watched many action movies, you've probably seen a modern-day take on the Ark of the Covenant. It's definitely one of the most well-known pieces of furniture in the Tabernacle. And it's the particular piece of furniture we will focus on in this chapter. The Ark of the Covenant speaks of Christ, our security. And after we speak of Christ, our security, we'll look at one more piece of furniture. That will be the mercy seat, or the throne, which speaks of Christ, our sovereign.

To set the stage for our study of the Ark of the Covenant, let's look at Exodus 25:10-16:

> "And they shall make an ark of acacia wood; two and a half cubits shall be its length, a cubit and a half its width, and a cubit and a half its height. And you shall overlay it with pure gold, inside and out you shall overlay it, and shall make on it a molding of gold all around. You shall cast four rings of gold for it, and put them in its four corners; two rings shall be on one side, and two rings on the other side. And you shall make poles of acacia wood, and overlay them with gold. You shall put the poles into the rings on the sides of the ark, that the ark may be carried by them. The poles shall be in

the rings of the ark; they shall not be taken from it. And you shall put into the ark the Testimony which I will give you."

Now, we're talking about the piece of furniture, which was a chest or a box sitting inside the Holy of Holies that was called the Ark or the Ark of the Covenant. Sometimes people get confused about the various arks in the Bible. If you were to ask most people what they thought an ark looked like, they might mention the story of Noah and the ark. However, this particular ark is not a boat. It is a chest for safe keeping, a repository in which someone would place something for safe keeping, for security. Yes. Noah built the ark as a place of safety. And Moses was once placed in a little ark made of bulrushes, which meant it was a place of safety. Somewhat similarly, the Ark of the Covenant speaks of security. It's a place for housing valuable assets. Additionally, as we continue to study, we will see that it is a marvelous picture of Christ, our security.

Truly, it's wonderful to be saved. But it's even more wonderful to know you're saved. It is even thrice wonderful to be saved, to know you're saved, and to know you can't lose your salvation. Isn't that the best? How great a salvation we have in the Lord Jesus Christ because He is our ark of safety. He is the person who keeps us secure.

Let's notice two major things about the Ark of the Covenant. First of all, we will see the construction of the ark. Secondly, we will look at the contents of the ark.

The Construction of the Ark of the Covenant

Notice Exodus 25:10a once again, "And they shall make an ark of acacia wood." Remember, the wood speaks of the humanity, the earthliness, of the Lord Jesus Christ. In Psalm 1:3, the Bible compares a righteous person to a tree. Also, in Isaiah 53, the Bible speaks of Jesus as a root out of dry ground.

Then we notice that not only was the ark of wood, but in Exodus 25:11a we notice the wood was overlaid with pure gold. "And you shall overlay it with pure gold, inside and out you shall overlay it." In the Bible, gold is symbolic of deity, royalty. So here we see both the deity of Christ and the humanity of Christ pictured and typified in this lovely Ark of the Covenant. Also, we see in Exodus 25:12 there are four rings in four corners. Four is the Earth number. The Bible speaks of the four angels in the four corners of the Earth, the four winds of the Earth, and so forth.

On the Ark of the Covenant are four corners. This tells me of the universality of our Savior: a corner pointing east, and a corner pointing west, a corner pointing north, and a corner pointing south. Jesus Christ is for all people—red, yellow, black, white; they are precious in His sight. I'm glad our salvation and our religion is not a provincial, parochial religion. I'm glad for its universality.

What about the poles? If you look in Exodus 25:13-14, you read, "And you shall make poles of acacia wood, and overlay them with gold. You shall put the poles into the rings on the sides of the ark, that the ark may be carried by them." These poles were long rods that were hooked through certain rings in each corner. Once the rods were attached, the priests could pick up the Ark easily and carry it. They were not to touch the Ark with their hands. Using the poles kept them from actually touching the Ark.

The Ark moved with them wherever they went; that is, it accompanied them. These poles speak of the availability of Christ. Indeed, He's always with me. Jesus is the friend that sticks closer than a brother.

The Contents of the Ark of the Covenant

Next, let's take some time to look at the contents of the Ark of the Covenant. I think there are some wonderful truths for us to learn. Look first at Exodus 25:16, "And you shall put into the ark the Testimony which I will give you." Also notice Hebrews 9:3-5 to see more clearly the three items God delineated for the contents of the ark:

> "And behind the second veil, the part of the tabernacle which is called the Holiest of All, which had the golden censer and the ark of the covenant overlaid on all sides with gold, in which were the golden pot that had the manna, Aaron's rod that budded, and the tablets of the covenant; and above it were the cherubim of glory overshadowing the mercy seat. Of these things we cannot now speak in detail."

First, in the Ark, we see the golden pot of manna. Second, we see Aaron's rod that budded. And finally, we see the tablets of the covenant, the stone tablets on which the Ten Commandments were written. These were in the Ark of the Covenant for security.

With these items in mind, remember, just as the ark speaks of safekeeping, it also speaks of Christ. There are certain things that are secure to us, kept for us, in Christ. To begin with, in Christ, we have resources. My resources are secure in Christ because manna spoke to them of a perpetual resource. As the Jewish people were in the desert, the Lord was providing for them. He was taking care of them. They had no farms. They had no dairies. They had no ways to produce the food they needed for sustenance, but daily the Lord was their resource.

Daily the manna came down from Heaven. That manna was a picture of the Lord Jesus Christ. Here are some ways that manna pictured the Lord Jesus Christ:

- It was small—that spoke of the humility of Christ.
- It was round—that spoke of the perfection of Christ.
- It was white—that spoke of the purity of Christ.
- It had the taste like a coriander seed—that spoke of the health-giving proprieties and the fragrance of Christ.
- It had the taste of oil—that symbolized the Holy Spirit that Jesus Christ gives.
- It had the taste of honey—that speaks of the sweetness of Christ.
- It came down from Heaven—that speaks of the heaven-sent source. The Lord Jesus is that bread that came down from Heaven.

Manna was a picture of the Lord Jesus Christ, and they fed upon Jesus Christ in type and in symbol. Day after day after day, they were provided for. As a reminder that God had given them this provision, they had to pick some of that manna up from the ground. Picking up this manna pictures the resurrection of Jesus—being lifted up from the ground and also His ascension. The manna was placed in the golden pot inside the Ark of the Covenant, and there it was preserved forever fresh. This action pictures the Lord Jesus Christ; the bread that came down from Heaven, now lifted up from the Earth, and now in glory still providing for His people.

We can be assured that our resource is in Christ. Just as He fed those people so long ago, day by day in that wilderness, I want you to know, day by day He takes care of us in this wilderness. God will take care of us! Isn't it great to know that as they came out of Egypt under the blood, that we've come out of this old-world system under the blood of Jesus? Just as He provided for them so long ago in type, He provides for us in reality. You and I are secure in our resource, who is Jesus.

Not only are we secure in His resources, but we are also secure in His resurrection. We understand security by looking at the second item located in the Ark of the Covenant. It's Aaron's rod which budded. This rod pictures the resurrection of Jesus Christ.

Now, let's think about how Aaron's rod happened to bud and who Aaron was. As you may recall, Aaron was the high priest of Israel. Look at Numbers 17 to see more of his story. In this chapter, you'll find something interesting. Some people rose up against Moses and Aaron. Moses was God's commander-in-chief; Aaron was God's high priest. But the people rebelled against their leadership and began to question them. God judged the people very severely because of their rebellion against His anointed priest because that anointed priest was a picture of Jesus.

Every Old Testament priest pre-figured Jesus, the great High Priest who ever lives to make intercession for us. That's the reason I'm not a priest today in the classical sense. I'm a preacher. A priest is someone who goes to God for you; a preacher is someone who tells you what Jesus has already done for you. We don't need a priest; we need a preacher to proclaim Jesus, the great High Priest, who has passed into the heavens. But every Old Testament priest was a picture of Jesus Christ, the fulfillment. Indeed, Aaron was a picture of Jesus Christ. When the people rebelled against Aaron, their rebellion was symbolic of people today who rebel against the Lord Jesus Christ. The judgment of God in their day pictures the judgment God's going to send upon anybody in this day who refuses the Lord Jesus Christ.

As the people began to question their leadership, God spoke to Moses about it all. God said to Moses, in effect, "Moses, we'll prove who is to be the leader, and I want you to show the people whom I've chosen as leader. Here's the way we're going to do it. I want you to go to the heads of the twelve tribes of Israel."

Then God said, "I want you to get a rod from every one of them." A rod is simply a stick. It's a plain, dead stick. God told Moses, "Get one from each of the leaders of the twelve tribes of the children of Israel. Each one will have his name put on the side of that rod. We'll have twelve of them."

Then God said, in effect, "We're going to go take them and put them in the tabernacle. We're going to leave them in there and then we're going to come back the next day."

God essentially said, "I'm going to show you, because of what's going to happen, whom I have chosen as my leader." And so, they did that.

You can read this account in Numbers 17:2-10:

> "Speak to the children of Israel, and get from them a rod from each father's house, all their leaders according to their fathers' houses—twelve rods. Write each man's name on his rod. And you shall write Aaron's name on the rod of Levi. For there shall be one rod for the head of each father's house. Then you shall place them in the tabernacle of meeting before the Testimony, where I meet with you. And it shall be that the rod of the man whom I choose will blossom; thus I will rid Myself of the complaints of the children of Israel, which they make against you."

> So Moses spoke to the children of Israel, and each of their leaders gave him a rod apiece, for each leader according to their fathers' houses, twelve rods; and the rod of Aaron was among their rods. And Moses placed the rods before the LORD in the tabernacle of witness.

> Now it came to pass on the next day that Moses went into the tabernacle of witness, and behold, the rod of Aaron, of the house of Levi, had sprouted and put forth buds, had produced blossoms and yielded ripe almonds. Then Moses brought out all the rods from before the LORD to all the children of Israel; and they looked, and each man took his rod.

> And the LORD said to Moses, "Bring Aaron's rod back before the Testimony, to be kept as a sign against the rebels, that you may put their complaints away from Me, lest they die."

Now, I've never seen a dead stick do that. Have you? It would be a miracle if you put your broom in your closet tonight and then came back in the morning to find it with leaves and flowers all over it. In Aaron's story, all of the other rods were still just dead sticks, but Aaron's rod had blossomed and bloomed. It had the bud, the flower, and the fruit all at the same time. What is this a picture of? It's a picture of the resurrection of Jesus Christ. You see that rod in the Ark of the Covenant pictures Christ, our resurrection, and Christ, our life. Because not only is Jesus Christ my resource; He is my source. He is my life.

Notice this same picture in Isaiah 53:2. "For he shall grow up before Him as a tender plant, and as a root out of dry ground. He has no form or comeliness; and when we see Him, there is no beauty that we should desire Him." Jesus is like a root out of a dry ground. In other words, Jesus is like a stick, a branch that grows out of the dry ground. But when it grew out of the dry ground, it had life in it. It wouldn't have grown if it hadn't had life. Jesus came to this Earth full of life because He was born of a virgin—perfect in every respect.

Also notice Isaiah 53:8, "He was taken from prison and from judgment, and who will declare His generation? For He was cut off from the land of the living; for the transgressions of My people He was stricken." Just like you would take a pair of garden shears and cut off a branch that had come up out of the ground, so also Jesus Christ was cut off.

Aaron's rod is a picture of Christ. One day out in the wilderness there was something in the wilderness that grew up, and Aaron saw that one day. He said, "Everybody ought to have a rod to lean on, something to hit rocks with. We all need something to kill snakes with and something to lean on." So, Aaron cut off the stick. The minute he cut it off, the source of life was cut off. That's exactly what happened to the Lord Jesus Christ. He was a rod and He was cut off.

Oh, but I want you to notice something wonderful. Look at Isaiah 53:10, "Yet it pleased the LORD to bruise Him; He has put Him to grief. When You make His soul an offering for sin, He shall see His seed, He shall prolong His days, and the pleasure of the LORD shall prosper in His hand." Now, what is this? Jesus is dead, and yet His days are prolonged. He's dead, and yet He's going to see His descendants. Why is that? Because God has given life to this dead rod—a picture of the resurrection of the Lord Jesus Christ.

The resurrection of Jesus was typified and pictured there in the Book of Numbers. Aaron's rod that budded speaks of Christ. The buds speak of His life; the blossoms speak of His beauty; and the almonds speak of His fruitfulness and the fruit of the Spirit. All of this is in the Lord Jesus Christ. So, not only is Christ my resource, but Christ is my resurrection. Our supply is secure.

There is one last thing that I want you to notice. Jesus is our righteousness. We see this symbolized in the last valuable treasure stored in the Ark of the Covenant—the stone tablets containing the Ten Commandments. Truly, Christ kept the law perfectly. He was the only one who kept it. Therefore, the law is put in the Ark of the Covenant. The stone tablets of the Ten Commandments symbolize the righteousness that God demands. Notice Romans 10:4, "For Christ is the end of the law for righteousness to everyone who believes." You see, Christ is the end of the law for righteousness. Christ is my righteousness, not the Ten Commandments. He's the only one who kept the Ten Commandments. Not me. Not you. Not anyone else.

You and I are not saved by keeping the law. Instead, we are saved through Christ. Jesus kept the law and then He died for us. In 2 Corinthians 5:21, we read, "For He made Him who knew no sin to be sin for us, that we might become the righteousness of God in Him."

Another interesting thing to notice about the Ark is something unusual. The stone tablet that was kept in the Ark of the Covenant was broken in two. Do you remember when this happened? Moses broke the stone tablet when he came down from the mountain and got upset with what God's people were doing.

They put the broken law into the Ark. However, on top of the broken tablets was a golden lid which closed the Ark. The lid on top of the Ark was called "the mercy seat." As the priest would offer a sacrifice, the blood would be sprinkled right on top of that golden lid, over the broken tablets. The broken tablets and broken laws were under the blood.

In Christ, our sins are under the blood. Jesus fulfilled it all, for "He made Him who knew no sin to be sin for us" (2 Corinthians 5:21a). Our sins have been atoned for and we are covered by and in His blood!

That Time When the Ark Was Stolen

As we close this chapter, I want to show you one more interesting story about the Ark of the Covenant. Let's look in 1 Samuel at a time when it was stolen. The Philistines took it, and they thought they had a treasure, but they had trouble.

The Ark actually caused them so much trouble. It caused problems everywhere they took it. Finally, they said, "Man, let's get rid of this." They said, "We want to get this off our hands." So, the Philistines took the Ark of the Covenant and hooked it to some cows and said, "Take it back." When the cows got as far as Beth Shemesh with the Ark, some farmers got curious about what was inside. They had heard the prohibitions about touching the Ark, but their carnal curiosity took over and they took the lid off the Ark. When they looked inside, they died instantly! God smote them!

If you look in 1 Samuel 6:19, you will read this part of the story. "Then He struck the men of Beth Shemesh, because they had looked into the ark of the LORD. He struck fifty thousand and seventy men of the people, and the people lamented because the LORD had struck the people with a great slaughter."

What does this picture? It typifies, to me, the condition we would all be in when the blood is removed from the broken law. The men of Beth Shemesh took away the mercy seat. They took away, as it were, the blood. And there is just the broken law. When the broken law is exposed, without being covered by the blood, there is judgment. We can thank God for the mercy seat. We can thank God for the blood that makes atonement for our souls. And I'm so glad I'm secure in Christ. I'm glad that in Christ is the manna that is my resource. I'm so grateful for the rod which represents my resurrection. I'm so thankful for the broken law that is covered by the blood which represents my righteousness found in Christ alone.

Let's pray together as we close this chapter:

Father, we thank You for this study of the tabernacle. We're thankful, Lord, for Christ, who is not only our sacrifice, but Christ who is our security. Lord, I pray if there's somebody whose transgression of the law is not under the blood, that they might come and let Christ be their security. For we pray in His name. Amen.

CHAPTER TEN

The Mercy Seat: A Picture of Jesus

It's such a glorious thing to know that God lives in us, that He rules from a throne of grace called a mercy seat.
—Adrian Rogers

After several chapters spent looking at the seven pieces of furniture, today we come to the final piece. This climatic piece is the mercy seat. The mercy seat was a slab of pure beaten gold that was two and one-half cubits by one and one-half cubits in dimension. As discussed in the previous chapter, it was a lid for the Ark of the Covenant. Some may think that the lid would be part of the Ark of the Covenant, but the Bible teaches this piece stood alone. It was not a part of the Ark; it was a separate piece of furniture altogether.

To discover more about the mercy seat, let's go to Exodus 25:17-22:

"You shall make a mercy seat of pure gold; two and a half cubits shall be its length and a cubit and a half its width. And you shall make two cherubim of gold; of hammered work you shall make them at the two ends of the mercy seat. Make one cherub at one end, and the other cherub at the other end; you shall make the cherubim at the two ends of it of one piece with the mercy seat. And the cherubim shall stretch out their wings above, covering the mercy seat with their wings, and they shall face one another; the faces of the cherubim shall be toward the mercy seat. You shall put the mercy seat on top of the ark, and in the ark you shall put the Testimony that I will give you. And there I will meet with you, and I will speak with you from above the mercy seat, from between the two cherubim which are on the ark of the Testimony, about everything which I will give you in commandment to the children of Israel."

Now, this mercy seat represents Christ, our sovereign. To prepare to study this final piece of furniture, let's review the other pieces of furniture.

The first piece of furniture was that brazen altar, which spoke of Christ, our sacrifice. The second piece of furniture, as you would enter into the outer court from the east, would be the laver. It was a wash basin made of brass, which symbolized the Word of God and Christ, our sanctification.

The next piece you would come to is a table and on that table would be some loaves of bread that were to be eaten by the priest. This bread was called showbread, and that pictured Christ, our sustenance. The fourth piece on the other side would be a lampstand to give light because there was no illumination by windows. All of the light of the tabernacle was from the golden lampstand, and that speaks of Christ, our sight. As you would proceed farther toward the Holy of Holies, you would come to the altar of incense that would represent Christ, our supplication. This is the case because the incense is a symbol of intercession and prayer. Inside the Holy of Holies, you came to the Ark of the Covenant, which was a chest. Remember, we said the Ark is a place for safekeeping, a place of reservoir; it speaks of Christ, our security.

The lid to the Ark of the Covenant was a throne. From that throne the Lord ruled. It was from that throne the Lord communed. It was there at that throne the Lord abode. That throne, or that seat, was called a mercy seat. It was where the Shekinah glory of God dwelt. The mercy seat was a picture of the Lord Jesus Christ, period.

Let's look at some New Testament verses just to point that out, so you'll see we're not forcing the meaning.

Other Verses That Teach About the Mercy Seat

To start with, let's look at Romans 3:24-25a, "Being justified freely by His grace through the redemption that is in Christ Jesus, Whom [that is, Christ Jesus] God set forth as a propitiation by His blood, through faith." The word "propitiation" is a Greek word, and it's translated mercy seat. That's literally what it means—mercy seat. God set Jesus Christ forth to be a mercy seat. "Hilasterion" is the Greek word that simply means mercy seat. So, Jesus Christ is a mercy seat. Whenever you see the word "propitiation" in the Bible, you can just say mercy seat. It means exactly the same thing.

Next, look at 1 John 4:10, "In this is love, not that we loved God, but that He loved us and sent His Son to be the propitiation for our sins." The mercy seat is for our sins. And so, I want to say this mercy seat, beyond the shadow of any doubt, speaks of the Lord Jesus Christ.

This mercy seat was over the Ark. As you may remember, inside the Ark were the tablets of stone that were broken. These symbolized the broken law. The gold on the mercy seat symbolized the royal deity of our Lord. Also, there was blood sprinkled on the mercy seat, and God in His Shekinah glory would cover right over the blood-sprinkled seat. You see, God would not see the broken law. All He would see would be the blood of atonement. That's the reason when He said, "When I see the blood, I will pass over you," (Exodus 12:13).

A Sunday school teacher was teaching on the omnipotence of God, and she asked her class, "Is there anything God cannot do?"

One little girl raised her hand, and said, "Yes, teacher, there's one thing God cannot do."

The teacher responded, "There is? What is that?"

The girl said, "God cannot see my sin through the blood of Jesus Christ."

And that's right. That's true.

You see, there's the broken law, there's the mercy seat, but sprinkled on that throne is blood. Once a year on the Day of Atonement, the high priest would go out to the brazen altar and take the blood of the burnt offering. He would then go into the Holy of Holies and sprinkle the blood on the mercy seat. Now, that pictured what Jesus would do one day.

You remember when Jesus had been raised from the grave and and Mary came into the garden? When she saw Jesus, she wanted to fall down and worship Jesus and kiss His feet. Do you remember that story? How did Jesus answer her? He said, "Do not cling to Me, for I have not yet ascended to My Father" (John 20:17a). What does all that mean? Because just a little later, in Luke 24:39, He said to His disciples, "Handle Me and see." What was the difference? One time He says to Mary, "Do not cling to Me, for I have not yet ascended to My Father." Then, another time, "Handle me, see me, touch me, feel me."

What's the difference? When the high priest prepared and washed himself and made atonement with the blood, he was not to be touched. He was not to be defiled by anybody because he was set apart as sacred, as holy, as separate from sinners. The high priest was going into the Holy of Holies to make atonement for the sin with blood in a basin.

Do you know what Jesus did when He ascended to Heaven? Jesus raised from the grave and ascended to Heaven. Then, He came back and appeared to the disciples and asked them to handle Him. But in that interval, He went to Heaven, and He sprinkled His blood there upon the mercy seat in the glory. That's what He did.

Notice Hebrews 9:12 to see this truth, "Not with the blood of goats and calves, but with His own blood He entered the Most Holy Place once for all, having obtained eternal redemption." That's what Jesus did! He sprinkled His blood upon the mercy seat there in Heaven. There's power in that blood. I just thank God for that blood that's sprinkled upon the mercy seat.

When you look also at Hebrews 4:14-16, all of this fits together like a beautiful mosaic and it'll bless your heart when you understand these truths. The Bible says,

> Seeing then that we have a great High Priest who has passed through the heavens, Jesus the Son of God, let us hold fast our confession. For we do not have a High Priest who cannot sympathize with our weaknesses, but was in all points tempted as we are, yet without sin. Let us therefore come boldly to the throne of grace, that we may obtain mercy and find grace to help in time of need.

Remember this: that in the tabernacle, the throne was not a throne of grace; it was a throne of judgment. If any one of those Jews had lifted up the flap of that veil and had gone into that Holy of Holies and looked upon the Ark of the Covenant, just like that they would have been killed. Indeed, no one would have dared to have the audacity to go into the Holy of Holies where the Shekinah glory of God dwelt unless he was the high priest and coming with blood. But now, Jesus has made the way for us. Jesus has gone in for us. Jesus has sprinkled His blood. That's all done. The blood is in glory now.

Look at Hebrews 4:16, "Let us therefore come boldly to the throne of grace, that we may obtain mercy and find grace to help in time of need." It's amazing! The judgment seat now becomes a mercy seat. The throne of judgment becomes a throne of grace. Because of the blood, we can come boldly to the throne. It's wonderful to know that we can come to God without a priest. You don't need a priest; you need a preacher.

We are our own priests. Jesus is our High Priest. We come to Him through the blood of Jesus. He's no farther from me than my knees are from the floor. The Bible teaches us in 1 Timothy 2:5, "For there is one God and one Mediator between God and men, the Man Christ Jesus." You and I can come boldly to the throne of grace. Glory to God. It's a wonderful salvation!

Now, let's see if we can make some applications about the mercy seat.

Application Question One: Where Does God Live?

Sometimes people ask, "Where on Earth does God Live?"

We said the tabernacle was but a pattern of the human body. The tabernacle had three rooms: the outer court, the inner court, and the innermost court (or the Holy of Holies). Man also is a house of three rooms. The tabernacle is a picture of man, as well as a picture of Christ, the perfect Man.

The outer court of the tabernacle pictures the body because the body is the place of sacrifice. We're to present our bodies a living sacrifice. They made the sacrifice of these animals in the outer court.

Then there is the inner court, where the priests met and communed and fellowshipped and worshipped. This corresponds to the soul, the innermost, the inner man. It's in our souls that we have fellowship with one another. We know each other on this level through our souls.

But the innermost court, that cube building, that Holy of Holies, represents the spirit of man. There's a difference in man's soul and man's spirit. The soul of man gives man self-consciousness and social consciousness, but the spirit of man gives God-consciousness.

Truly, God is spirit, and they that worship Him must worship Him in spirit and in truth (see John 4:24). The Holy of Holies in the tabernacle represents the human spirit. That's where God dwelt.

Do you know where God dwells in me? God dwells in my spirit. He says, "I will dwell in the high and holy place with him who has a contrite and humble spirit" (Isaiah 57:15).

God has been moving in and out of houses. The first house God lived in was a house of three rooms named Adam. But when Adam sinned, God moved out, for God won't live in a dirty house. Adam died immediately. He didn't die physically or psychologically; he died spiritually. And to be spiritually dead is to be minus God in the spirit. God moved out.

The next house that God lived in was the tabernacle as we just read. God said, I'll dwell right there between the cherubim right over the mercy seat. But even that house became defiled after the tabernacle became the temple.

Remember what Jesus said in Matthew 21:13, "It is written, 'My house shall be called a house of prayer,' but you have made it a 'den of thieves.'" Then Jesus moved out. God moved out. The Holy Spirit moved out. God saturated that place with His absence.

They didn't know it. Instead, they went on to worship. They trudged to temple every Sabbath day and they went in, but God was nowhere around. Instead, God said, "See! Your house is left to you desolate" (Matthew 23:38). "My Father's house." That's what it was meant to be, but now He says, "your house." Rather than enjoying their salvation, they were just enduring religion. And so, that was God's pattern house.

But then, thank the Lord, there was God's perfect house. His name was Jesus!

God's primary house was Adam.

God's pattern house was the temple.

God's perfect house was Jesus.

The Bible says, in John 1:14a, "And the Word became flesh and dwelt among us [tabernacled among us]." Jesus was a tabernacle.

We also read about this in John 2:19, where Jesus said, "Destroy this temple, and in three days I will raise it up." Jesus was a temple. Jesus was a tabernacle. Jesus was a house of God—a house of three rooms. He was healthy in His body, He was happy in His soul, and He was holy in His Spirit. And here, He was the perfect man. Truly, "For in Him dwells all the fullness of the Godhead bodily" (Colossians 2:9).

Then, God moved out of that house, too, because that house became a dirty house, and God won't live in a dirty house. The Bible says, "For He made Him who knew no sin to be sin for us" (2 Corinthians 5:21a). "All we like sheep have gone astray...and the LORD has laid on Him the iniquity of us all" (Isaiah 53:6). My sin, your sin, our sin, and the sin of the world was put upon Jesus. When that was true, God the Father separated Himself from God the Son. It's not easy to understand, but it is what we believe. That's the reason Jesus hung on the cross and cried in Mark 15:34, "My God, My God, why have You forsaken Me?" God moved out because God won't live in a dirty house. And Jesus died on Calvary all alone.

Next, I want you to notice God's permanent house.

It's really this simple: God dwells in me permanently. He'll never move out of me. He'll never move out of you. Jesus Christ is now my mercy seat. The blood, one offering, is sprinkled forever on the mercy seat in Heaven. Jesus is that mercy seat. That throne of grace is a throne that is really not only in Heaven, but is also a throne in my heart because my body is a temple of the holy God. Just as the Ark of the Covenant was in the tabernacle, and just as the Ark of the Covenant was in that temple, Jesus Christ is in me and He will never, ever leave me. He'll never leave us!

Do you remember when Solomon's temple was dedicated? They brought the Ark into Solomon's temple and then they pulled the poles out of the Ark. All through the wilderness that Ark had been carried by those long poles. Once the Ark came into the temple, it was not to be moved anymore. It had found a permanent dwelling place. The glory of God hadn't filled the temple yet. But then when the priest backed out, the Bible says the glory of God filled that temple (see 2 Chronicles 5).

What does this picture when the Ark came into the temple? That pictured Christ coming into us. When the poles were pulled out, that pictures Christ always in us. When the priest backed out, that pictures Christ only in us. Christ always, Christ only. When it became Christ always, and Christ only, then the Bible says the glory of the Lord filled the house.

Do you want the glory of God to fill your body? Do you want God to fill you? Your body is the temple of the Holy Spirit, which you have of God. To allow God to fill you, just say, "Christ always, and Christ only." When Jesus Christ moves into you, He moves in never to move out again. That's the reason I believe in the eternal security of the believer. Jesus said, "And I will pray the Father, and He will give you another Helper, that He may abide with you forever" (John 14:16).

My heart is not a hotel with a check-out time of 10:00 a.m. on Monday morning. Instead, Jesus Christ lives in me forever. If you know Him, He lives in your heart forever as well.

Application Question Two: What Lessons Can We Learn?

There are some wonderful lessons about what we can learn from the mercy seat. Let me share five lessons that are true because Jesus Christ is our mercy seat. These are true because Christ is our sovereign, because Christ, the Ark of the Covenant, is in His holy temple, which is our bodies.

Lesson number one is the lesson concerning salvation. We need to teach people what salvation is. Sometimes we don't do a very good job of teaching about salvation. Salvation is not getting your sins forgiven. That just gets you ready for salvation. Salvation is not going to Heaven when you die. That's the result of salvation. Salvation is not getting man out of Earth into Heaven; it is getting God out of Heaven into man. Understand this.

Just as the Shekinah glory of God dwelt above that mercy seat, the glory of God dwells in me. Just as the Ark was in the temple, Jesus is in me. Do you understand what salvation is? It's getting God back into man. What happened to Adam that caused Adam to die? God moved out of Adam. What happens when a man gets saved? God moves back into him. There's the lesson concerning salvation, therefore. It's getting God back into man.

The second lesson I want you to learn is the lesson concerning spirituality. What is spirituality? Spirituality is having God in you at all times, at all places. Please don't act spiritual. God doesn't want you act spiritual. A person who acts spiritual is a hypocrite. You are spiritual, so you don't need to act. Jesus had a lot to say about the play actors; He called them hypocrites.

Have you ever noticed people come to church and suddenly get spiritual when they get inside the church building? And we say to our kids, "Now, kids, we're going to God's house, so you behave a certain way in God's house." This isn't God's house. I am God's house. You are God's house. Certainly, we ought to have reverence in church because of the purpose we've met. Yes, we ought to take care of our church buildings because they belong to God. Sure, your children should look nice for church, but the church building is not God's house. You and I are God's house.

Consider the words of 1 Corinthians 6:19-20, "Or do you not know that your body is the temple of the Holy Spirit who is in you, whom you have from God and you are not your own? For you were bought with a price; therefore glorify God in your body and in your spirit, which are God's."

So, what is spirituality? Spirituality is not suddenly getting a pious tone when you come to church. Every day is a holy day. Every place is a sacred place. And God does not dwell in temples made with hands. Your body is the temple of the Holy Spirit of God. When a person is saved, he doesn't suddenly start acting religious under certain circumstances. He is spiritual twenty-four hours a day. In all natural things he's to be spiritual, and in all spiritual things he's to be natural. He's naturally supernatural and supernaturally natural. Does that make sense? You are to be the same every day, and that is holy.

People say, "Do you keep the Sabbath?"

I say, "I sure do. I keep it Sunday, Monday, Tuesday, Wednesday, Thursday, Friday, Saturday, and Sunday again. Every day is a Sabbath day. Every day is a day to rest in Jesus. Every day is a holy place. Every place is a place of service."

We are to be spiritual all the time. You won't get sudden quivers in your voice when you talk spiritually. When you let the Lord fill you with His Spirit, He's going to give you a pleasing personality. You're not going to be some religious psycho jumping around with buggy eyes. You're going to be natural, but you're going to be supernaturally natural and naturally supernatural.

You know the way I test my friends? When I'm off at a convention, I get in a motel room with one of my preacher buddies. They talk the same way they talk when they're standing right here in this pulpit. They don't turn it on and turn it off. They don't have one kind of behavior one place and another kind of behavior another place. It's the same way all the time. That's the way it ought to be.

Also, let's review the lesson from the mercy seat concerning security. Christ rules from a throne—the mercy seat. The mercy seat is upon the Ark, which represents Christ. My body represents the temple. The Ark is in the temple, never to be taken out again. The lesson: Christ abides with me forever; I'm secure.

Some people don't believe in eternal security. They think they're going to get in Heaven and then they're going to be secure. They don't think they are secure down here. I've said it before and I'll say it again: If you're not secure down here, you won't be secure up there. Security is not in a place; it's in a person.

What makes you think that just because you slam the door behind you in Heaven, you're going to be safe? Remember, some of the angels fell from Heaven.

I want to share something, friend. I had rather be a saved sinner than an innocent angel. I had rather be a saved sinner than Adam in the Garden of Eden before he'd ever sinned. Adam was only innocent. I am positively righteous. Adam could sin and lose his fellowship with God. I can sin, but I can't lose my relationship with God.

There is nothing that can separate me from God. And if I sin, God will whip the daylights out of me if I don't confess it, but I'm still His child. "For whom the LORD loves He chastens, and scourges every son whom He receives" (Hebrews 12:6). But I am His child forever and ever because the mercy seat is there, the blood is upon it, the Ark of the Covenant is in the temple, the poles have been removed, and He's not moving out again. I am His temple.

In addition, I want to share the lesson concerning soul winning. What is soul winning? If man is a house of three rooms—body, soul, and spirit—and if the spirit of man is that which needs to be regenerated, the devil will move heaven and earth to get churches to feed man's body and to educate man's mind in lieu of converting man's spirit.

Often, people will come to us at church concerned about global starvation. They want us to take the assets of the missions and evangelism ministry and put it into feeding hungry mouths. Certainly, I believe people need to be fed. But let me quickly add, if you feed people without giving them the Gospel, you prolong their lives, you prolong their productivity. But until Jesus comes, everybody living is going to die. Giving people food without giving them the Gospel is the devil's plan. Educating people without giving them the Gospel simply makes them clever devils. Our job is to get the Gospel out.

We need to be very careful because we can be made to look hard-hearted, or we can be made to look like we don't care about the needs of man. However, I want to tell you the devil knows that it doesn't matter what you do to the minds and bodies of people if their hearts are not changed. The devil doesn't want the spirit of man to be born again. When Adam died, he died immediately in the spirit, progressively in his soul, ultimately in his body. When man gets saved, he is justified immediately in his spirit, sanctified progressively in his soul, glorified ultimately in his body. But the devil would try to get you to leapfrog over the Spirit and start with the soul or the body. He doesn't want people coming to know Christ.

Another lesson we glean from the mercy seat is the lesson concerning service. Recently, I was reading Hudson Taylor's book called the "Spiritual Secret." If you haven't, you ought to read it. Hudson Taylor was the founder of the China Inland Mission. When he first got saved, he started out wanting God to do things for him. And then after he grew a little, he wanted to do things for God. But as he grew more, he decided God wanted to do something through him. Now, have you learned that lesson?

Service is not you doing something for God; it is God doing something in you and through you. God lives in me. God lives in you.

Do you know when God preaches through me? When I get myself out of the way and just let Him speak through me. You say, "Well, now, Adrian, you think God is speaking through you when sometimes you say something humorous? Don't you think that's Adrian?" I would have to answer, "Not necessarily."

Honestly, I believe that God made us, every one of us, unique individuals. He wants us to be the same everywhere, loving Him, acting just as we would act—not our worst selves, but ourselves, our best selves. Also, God has a sense of humor. God has a sense of intrigue. God has a sense of order. God has a sense of compassion. God has all of this.

God takes our personalities and uses us accordingly. Once God chooses us, He uses us the way we are created. God takes a person who is himself, filled with the Holy Spirit, and then God uses that man's thoughts, God uses that man's mind, God uses that man's or that woman's gestures, whatever it is. God uses that to communicate truth.

It's not what we're doing for God, even though it may seem very human. It's what God is doing through us.

And if we could learn just to say, "Lord, You take my mind, take my hands, take my feet. Take whatever I have, take my reading, take my logic, take whatever it is, Lord, and You use it." God will use it.

Closing Thoughts on the Mercy Seat

The Ark of the Covenant dwelt in the temple. That represents Jesus. And He dwells in us. He rules from a throne called the mercy seat. The Shekinah glory of God hovers over it. The sprinkled blood is interposed between Himself and the broken law.

It's such a glorious thing to know that God lives in us, that He rules from a throne of grace called a mercy seat.

Let's pray together as we close this chapter:

Father, we thank You so much that Christ lives in us and that He wants to speak through us. And that, Lord, we didn't just get our sins forgiven, but we received You. Lord, You are not finished with us yet. You're making us day by day what You want us to be. And we thank You for this, Lord. We thank You, Lord, that we've been immediately justified in our Spirits, but that You're progressively sanctifying us in our souls. And we thank You, Lord, that one day You'll ultimately glorify us in our bodies, even as the body of Jesus was glorified. You change our vile bodies like unto Your glorious body. We thank You and we praise You for that. Seal the truth of this lesson to our hearts. For we pray in His name. Amen.

CHAPTER ELEVEN

A Well-Dressed Priest: Christ, Our High Priest

Because Christ is our High Priest, it is through Christ that we're all made to be a kingdom of priests.
—Adrian Rogers

O ver the past few chapters, we have been systematically looking at the pieces of furniture in the tabernacle. We've had the chance to study each particular piece in detail and consider its significance. Let's change gears a little and look at Aaron the priest and how he was to be dressed for service in the tabernacle. He was incredibly well-dressed and clothed in a most particular fashion. You can see what he was wearing in Exodus 28:31-35:

> "You shall make the robe of the ephod all of blue. There shall be an opening for his head in the middle of it; it shall have a woven binding all around its opening, like the opening in a coat of mail, so that it does not tear. And upon its hem you shall make pomegranates of blue, purple, and scarlet, all around its hem, and bells of gold between them all around: a golden bell and a pomegranate, a golden bell and a pomegranate, upon the hem of the robe all around. And it shall be upon Aaron when he ministers, and its sound will be heard when he goes into the holy place before the LORD and when he comes out, that he may not die."

Now, if Aaron, the high priest, would have had the audacity to worship the Lord without being properly dressed, he would have been killed on the spot. What he wore to worship was significant. What about for us today? Are we dressed to worship? I don't care where you bought your clothes or what color they are or that sort of thing. Of course, you understand that is not what I'm talking about. I want you to understand the spiritual application of the truth.

The garments the high priest wore had a great spiritual application. The high priest in the Old Testament is a picture of the Christian in the New Testament. The high priest in the Old Testament was a picture of Christ, but he's also a picture of the believer. Because Christ is our High Priest, it is through Christ that we're all made to be a kingdom of priests.

Just as the tabernacle was a picture of Christ and also a blueprint of the believer, the high priest was a picture of Christ and also symbolized the saints. The Bible tells us in 1 Peter 2:9a, "You are a chosen generation, a royal priesthood." And so, I don't know whether you've ever seen a priest before or not, but I am one. And you are a priest if you're saved. The Lord has made us all to be priests unto Him. Because we are His priests, we have the right to come before Him to minister.

Just as Aaron, the high priest in the Old Testament, went through that outer court into the inner court and then into the innermost court—the Holy of Holies, the very presence of God—we can do that, too. Isn't that wonderful? Any believer can go into the Holy of Holies if he's properly dressed.

Let's look at Hebrews 10:19-23:

> Therefore, brethren, having boldness to enter the Holiest by the blood of Jesus, by a new and living way which He consecrated for us, through the veil, that is, His flesh, and having a High Priest over the house of God, let us draw near with a true heart in full assurance of faith, having our hearts sprinkled from an evil conscience and our bodies washed with pure water. Let us hold fast the confession of our hope without wavering, for He who promised is faithful.

The Bible teaches Aaron took the blood of animals and went into the Holy of Holies when he was properly dressed. So also, we can take the blood of Jesus as our sacrifice and come boldly through the torn veil, which is His body, right into the Holy of Holies and commune with the Lord.

So, how do we get properly dressed for entering the Holy of Holies? The answer comes from taking a closer look at Aaron's robe.

There are three things I want you to notice about Aaron's robe. First of all, I want you to notice that it speaks of the believer's position. Secondly, it speaks of the believer's profession. And lastly, Aaron's robe speaks of the believer's possession.

Aaron's Robe and the Believer's Position

Aaron's robe was made of linen. Though it was blue and beautiful and had bells and pomegranates all around it, it was made of linen for a very special reason. If Aaron dared to go in with a robe that was made of wool, he would have been slain. Instead, the Bible says very carefully that Aaron was to dress just exactly as God told him to dress or he would have been slain right on the spot. Why was Aaron's robe made of linen?

We find that answer in Ezekiel 44. God is speaking again about His priests who go into the sanctuary, and here God reveals why the priests wore linen. He doesn't tell us over in the Book of Exodus that I can find, just tells us that his garments are to be of linen, but God doesn't tell us why.

The best commentary I've found on the Bible is the Bible, and you'd be surprised how much light the Bible will add to the context of a particular topic. Notice the instruction in Ezekiel 44:16-18.

> "They shall enter My sanctuary, and they shall come near My table to minister to Me, and they shall keep My charge. And it shall be, whenever they enter the gates of the inner court, that they shall put on linen garments; no wool shall come upon them while they minister within the gates of the inner court or within the house. They shall have linen turbans on their heads and linen trousers on their bodies; they shall not clothe themselves with anything that causes sweat."

Here's the reason the priests could not wear wool. God said the priest needed to wear the cool, clean, crisp linen because, "they shall not clothe themselves with anything that causes sweat." If there could be an 11th commandment, it would be "Thou shalt not sweat it."

God does not want you ministering to Him in such a way as to cause sweat. The priest was dressed in a robe of linen; that is, he was to be cool and calm and collected as he ministered unto the Lord. Because of his sin, man began to perspire. In Genesis 3:19, God said to Adam as his judgment for sin, "In the sweat of your face you shall eat bread…" Man had work to do in the Garden of Eden, but it was not his work that produced sweat. Sweat represents man's effort. It represents man's toil. It represents man's labor.

When we come to Jesus, we cease from our own works, and we rest in the Lord Jesus Christ. Six days there was sweat, but on the seventh day there was none. Jesus Christ is our rest. Jesus Christ is our Sabbath. God doesn't want us to sweat it. He wants us to rest in Him.

The Bible says in Hebrews 4:10, "For he who has entered His rest has himself also ceased from his works as God did from His." Nobody can minister before the Lord, nobody can come before the Holy of Holies, nobody can come into the inner sanctum, and dwell in the light and bask in the Shekinah glory, until he stops trying to save himself by his sweat. He needs to rest in the finished work of the Lord Jesus Christ. No sweat. Sweat is the result of sin.

We don't come before Him with sweat; we come before Him with blood, and it's the blood of Jesus and not our own works. Oh, how wonderful when we realize, "For by grace you have been saved through faith" (Ephesians 2:8a).

Not only are we saved by grace, but we also serve by grace. Jesus Christ gave Himself for me, that He might give Himself to me, that He might live through me. So many people only have half a gospel. They come to Jesus to get their sins forgiven, but they fail to realize that not only are we saved, reconciled by His death; we are saved by His life.

Jesus Christ is alive, and He lives in me. He lives in you. He's alive in us, and He doesn't want us to do anything for Him. He wants to do something through us. Oh, how many people are offering sweat to God, and He doesn't want it. God says, in effect, "No sweat. You serve me in the unction and the power of the Holy Spirit and not in the carnality of your perspiration."

During the early years of my ministry, I started out trying to do things for God. It was one of the greatest discoveries of my life when I learned God didn't want what I could do for Him. Instead, He wanted me to get out of the way. He wanted me to be crucified with Christ so that He could take over and do something through me. Any praise for my life or my ministry has to be passed on to Calvary. It has to go to the Lord Jesus Christ because He's the One who does it. "I have been crucified with Christ; it is no longer I who live, but Christ lives in me" (Galatians 2:20a).

You know, it's wonderful to rest in Jesus. I feel sorry for people who are trying rather than trusting. I feel sorry for people who are sweating rather than resting in the finished work of the Lord Jesus Christ.

Are you properly dressed right now? If you're wearing wool, you're not. If you're wearing linen, you are. If you are coming dressed in the robe of His righteousness, resting in the finished work of Calvary, you are. If you have quit trying and started trusting, you are. If the old you is dead, and if Christ is now living through you, you are. If you are serving in the finished work of Calvary, you are. If you are resting in the finished work of Jesus, then you're properly dressed to come and serve the Lord.

Aaron's Robe and the Believer's Profession

The second thing I want you to notice about Aaron's robe is the believer's profession. The linen speaks of our position, which is one of righteousness and resting, but the bells on the robe speak of our profession. Look at Exodus 28:34. The Bible tells us that all around the bottom of the robe of the high priest, there was to be a border of bells and pomegranates. The Bible says, "A golden bell and a pomegranate, a golden bell and a pomegranate, upon the hem of the robe all around."

In Exodus 28:35, God says he's got to be dressed in linen or he'll die. To survive, Aaron needed to have these items attached to his robe—a bell and a pomegranate. If he doesn't have the bell, he's surely going to die. If the bells don't ring, the priest must die. When Aaron would go into the Holy of Holies with blood to offer upon the mercy seat, all the people were waiting in the outer court listening. As long as they could hear those bells ringing, they'd think *He's still alive. God's accepting the offering. It's all right.* But if the bells had stopped ringing, they would have said, "Oh no, God killed him. He died right in there. He tried to come into the presence of God, but the bells weren't ringing, and he died."

What does that speak of? If the linen represents our rest in Christ, the bells represent our profession of Christ. When a person trusts in the finished work of Calvary, then the very next thing, to prove that he means business, is that he begins to confess Christ. He'll ring the bells and tell the people.

With this in mind, let's look at Romans 10:9-10. You may know these verses by heart. The Bible says, "That if you confess with your mouth the Lord Jesus and believe in your heart that God has raised Him from the dead, you will be saved. For with the heart one believes unto righteousness, and with the mouth confession is made unto salvation."

What does this passage mean? It means, dear friend, that if you do not confess Christ, you're not believing with a Bible faith. The faith that will not lead to confession will not lead to Heaven.

Notice what Jesus said in Matthew 10:32-33 about the same subject, "Therefore whoever confesses Me before men, him I will also confess before My Father who is in heaven. But whoever denies Me before men, him I will also deny before My Father who is in heaven." Jesus said, "If you don't ring the bells down here, I'm not going to ring the bells up there."

If you will, notice the same thing in the Gospel of Mark: "For whoever is ashamed of Me and My words in this adulterous and sinful generation, of him the Son of Man also will be ashamed when He comes in the glory of His Father with the holy angels" (Mark 8:38).

Some people want to keep their relationship with Jesus a secret. They say, "I trust Jesus Christ to save me, but I'm not going to let these Christians know about it. I'm going to keep it a secret. I'm not going to make a public profession of my faith because I don't want anyone to know about it. I'm just going to keep to myself and remain private." But that's not how this works. We must wear the "bells." We must confess Christ!

Remember, the bells had to be upon the robe. With no robe, don't worry about the bells. I mean, it's no good for you to make a profession if you're not wearing the robe. The robe is resting in Jesus—the finished work of Calvary. That's the way the priests had to come.

But the robes without the bells are not enough. It's not enough for you to say that you're resting in Christ and that you're trusting Christ if you're not confessing Christ. Walking down the aisle doesn't save you. Shaking a preacher's hand doesn't save you. You're saved by faith in Christ. But faith without works is dead. And a man who says that he believes in Jesus Christ and keeps it a secret is simply deceiving himself. Jesus said in Matthew 10:33, "But whoever denies Me before men, him I will also deny before My Father who is in heaven."

The Bible also tells us in Romans 10:10, "For with the heart one believes unto righteousness, and with the mouth confession is made unto salvation." Similarly, Psalm 107:2 instructs us, "Let the redeemed of the LORD say so." Honestly, I have never known a real Christian who was ashamed to confess Jesus Christ. I'm not talking about in church. I'm talking about at the grocery and at the restaurant. I'm talking about in the hospital. I'm talking about in the office.

Those of us who are Christians better start ringing the bells. Confession without belief makes a person a hypocrite, but belief without confession is cowardly. Belief that is confessed makes one a true Christian. It is not the confession that saves; it's faith that saves. It is the confession that shows the faith and proves the faith. Faith gives you the fact of your salvation; confession gives you the feeling of your salvation. And if you've not been having the joy that you ought to have, why don't you ring the bells a little louder?

Aaron's Robe and the Believer's Possession

There's one last thing I want you to notice about Aaron's robe. Not only the believer's position—resting in Christ. Not only the believer's profession—confessing Christ or ringing the bells. But I want you to notice, finally, the believer's possession—his fruit.

Go back, if you will, to Exodus 28:33. The Bible says, "And upon its hem you shall make pomegranates of blue, purple, and scarlet, all around its hem, and bells of gold between them all around." God says there's to be a balance. There is to be the bell and then there is to be the fruit, and then there is to be the bell and then there is to be the fruit. Indeed, there are some folks who simply ring the bells, but they don't bear the fruit, and there are some people who purport to produce the fruit, but they don't ring the bells. The fruit pictures what we are. You see, not only are we to ring the bells and tell the people; we're to wear the fruit and show the people. When we're resting in the Lord Jesus Christ, there are two distinct manifestations. One is testimony; the other is fruit.

If testimony and fruit are not there, you're not a real priest. You're not a well-dressed priest. You're not ready to worship. You're not ready to come into the Holy of Holies. You are to be ringing the bells. You are to be showing the fruit. Wear the fruit and show the people; ring the bells and tell the people.

What is this fruit? It's described in Galatians 5:22-23, "But the fruit of the Spirit is love, joy, peace, longsuffering, kindness, goodness, faithfulness, gentleness, self-control. Against such there is no law." Now, notice it doesn't say the "fruits" of the Spirit. So many people think these are nine fruits. Someone may believe there's some of the fruit I have and some of the fruit I don't have. Don't kid yourself. These are not nine fruits; this is one fruit with nine flavors. Scripture doesn't say, "The fruits of the Spirit are…" It says, "The fruit of the Spirit is…." These are nine characteristics that are manifested in the life of every Spirit-filled believer.

Never confuse the gifts of the Spirit with the fruit of the Spirit. One person may have the gift of mercy and another person may have the gift of ministry. Another person may have the gift of miracles and another may have the gift of healing. One may have the gift of prophecy and another may have the gift of tongues or interpretation. But with fruit, the Bible teaches there is one singular fruit that is to be in all of our lives. This is the fruit of the Spirit. Do we have this fruit? Do I? Do you? It is to be present in all our lives.

Closing Thoughts About Aaron's Robe

Are you ready to worship? Are you well dressed? Are the bells there? Is the fruit there? Is anything missing? I talk to some people who tell me they really love Jesus. But there's no fruit in their lives. So, nobody believes them. Because there is no real fruit in their lives, they have no real impact on the people around them. They tell everyone they love the Lord, but no one trusts their testimony. On the other hand, I've met people who are all fruit and no bells. They have the mistaken idea, "Well, I just want people to see my life. I know I don't witness like I ought to, but you know what my philosophy is? I just believe if I'll go in my office and live like a Christian, people will see the fruit of my life and they'll want Jesus."

Honestly, people are not saved by your life; they're saved by Jesus' death. It is Jesus' death that made your life possible. If you don't tell them what makes your life possible, you're masquerading under false pretenses and getting glory for something that's not yours.

You need to ring the bells and tell the people. You need to wear the fruit and show the people. You need to do both! And the whole time you're doing it, you're not sweating about it. There's no sweat. You don't have to act holy; you are holy! You don't have to try to be a Christian.

If this ever dawns on me and you, we're going to be some kind of powerhouse! This thing called Christianity is something glorious—to be able to come into the Holy of Holies, a royal priesthood.

Jesus Christ provides our position—that's resting.

Our profession—that's ringing.

Our possession—that's reproducing the fruit.

Let's pray together as we close this chapter:

Father, we're so grateful for these lessons on the tabernacle. Lord, they've been so rich and have been a blessing to us. Lord, I just believe that our world has so many people who are sweating it out rather than resting in Jesus. Father, I pray that You'd help us to rest in the finished work of Calvary. Now, Father, I know that none of us are resting as we ought, none of us are testifying as we should, and none of us have the fruit in perfection. Lord, we know that we're not going to be perfect until we meet You, but, Lord, we're thankful for the change that's there. As imperfect as our faith is, Lord, we're grateful for the evidence that we belong to Jesus Christ, and we praise You for it, and we pray in His name. Amen.

CHAPTER TWELVE

A Clean Conscience: Jesus, Our Cleansing Agent

The worst pollution of all is the pollution of the soul.
—Adrian Rogers

W hat is a clean conscience and how do we have one? Let's think about that as we begin this next chapter in our study of the tabernacle. To launch us into a conversation about having a clean conscience, let's look at Hebrews 9:11-15:

> But Christ came as High Priest of the good things to come, with the greater and more perfect tabernacle not made with hands, that is, not of this creation. Not with the blood of goats and calves, but with His own blood He entered the Most Holy Place once for all, having obtained eternal redemption. For if the blood of bulls and goats and the ashes of a heifer, sprinkling the unclean, sanctifies for the purifying of the flesh, how much more shall the blood of Christ, who through the eternal Spirit offered Himself without spot to God, cleanse your conscience from dead works to serve the living God? And for this reason He is the Mediator of the new covenant, by means of death, for the redemption of the transgressions under the first covenant, that those who are called may receive the promise of the eternal inheritance.

Let's think, as we're studying about the tabernacle, about what it means to have a good, clean conscience. Notice in verse 14: "How much more shall the blood of Christ, who through the eternal Spirit offered Himself without spot to God, cleanse your conscience from dead works to serve the living God?" Having read that, let's go back in the Old Testament to Numbers 19 for one of the most blessed studies I've ever done in my life. Get ready to learn some very wonderful truths about a clean conscience.

You know, the worst pollution of all is the pollution of the soul. Let's consider a wonderful object lesson found in Numbers 19, as it relates to Hebrews 9. Numbers 19 is a long chapter, and I want to point out the word "unclean." I want you to notice in this chapter that the word "unclean" is used, if my count is correct, at least 17 times:

- Verse 7, "...the priest shall be *unclean* until evening."
- Verse 8, "...and shall be *unclean* until evening."
- Verse 10, "...and be *unclean* until evening."
- Verse 11, "...shall be *unclean* seven days."
- Verse 13, "...He shall be *unclean*, because the water of purification was not sprinkled on him; his *uncleanness* is still on him."
- Verse 14, "...all who are in the tent shall be *unclean* seven days."
- Verse 15, "...which has no cover fastened on it, is *unclean*."
- Verse 16, "...or a grave, shall be *unclean* seven days."
- Verse 17, "And for an *unclean* person they shall take..."
- Verse 19, "The clean person shall sprinkle the *unclean* on the third day and..."
- Verse 20, "But the man who is *unclean* and does not purify himself..." and "The water of purification has not been sprinkled on him; he is *unclean*."
- Verse 21, "...the water of purification shall be *unclean* until evening."
- Verse 22, "Whatever the *unclean* person touches shall be *unclean* and the person who touches it shall be *unclean* until evening."

I suppose you might call this the "dirty chapter." But it's not really that. For all the Word of God is clean, but it deals with dirt. Unclean, unclean, unclean, unclean, unclean, unclean, unclean,

unclean, unclean, unclean. This whole chapter is dealing with being unclean. But He's not talking about microbes. He's not talking about dirt. He's talking about ceremonial uncleanliness. The other word that it repeatedly used in Numbers 19 is the word "death" or "dead." And God is linking uncleanness with death.

Now, uncleanliness or uncleanness stands for a state of mind and a state of soul and a state of spirit that is not right with God, and it stands for sin. Sin makes us unclean. What is God saying in Numbers chapter 19? He's saying that death and sin or death and uncleanness are inseparably linked. Sin causes death, and death, therefore, is the visible sign of sin.

Often, we talk about and pray for the families of people who have died. Sometimes we talk about people who die of sickness and then we talk about other people who die a natural death. May I tell you there is no such thing as a natural death. All death is unnatural. It's not what God planned for us. All death is the result of sin, not necessarily your personal sin, but had there been no sin there'd have been no death. There was no sin in the Garden of Eden until sin came. "For the wages of sin is death" (Romans 6:23a).

Indeed, "The soul who sins shall die" (Ezekiel 18:20a). Death and sin are inseparably linked. God uses death ceremonially in the Old Testament as an object lesson and a symbol of sin. Keeping this in mind, I want you to notice what God was saying here in Numbers 19 when God is giving injunctions over and over again about not touching a dead body.

When God told these primitive people not to touch a dead body, He was trying to keep them from getting germs. God was trying to keep them from catching contagious diseases that might have caused the death. But He was doing more than that. He was teaching a theological and a ceremonial lesson. God was teaching that just as a person, for hygiene's sake, would stay away from that which is dead and that which corrupts, He's saying for moral and spiritual hygiene we need to stay away from sin. When God said, "Don't touch a dead body," He was doing more than giving a lesson in hygiene. He was saying by that object lesson, "Don't pollute your soul with sin."

Here's the important thing to remember—death symbolizes sin. Death and sin are inseparably linked. And so, as we think about soul pollution in this chapter, I want you to think with me along three lines: the causes of soul pollution, the consequences of soul pollution, and the cleansing of soul pollution. Or we might put it this way: the causes of an unclean conscience, the consequences of an unclean conscience, and the cleansing of an unclean conscience.

The Causes of an Unclean Conscience

What would cause a person back in this ancient time to become polluted? Look at Numbers 19:11: "He who touches the dead body of anyone shall be unclean seven days." If a man walked into a room where someone had just died and reached out to touch the dead body, he would be unclean for seven days. Under the Levitical system, back when the tabernacle was set up and operating, this was the law.

Remember that death represents sin. Sin and death are inseparably linked in the Bible. Deliberately touching a dead body was a sin. The people in the Old Testament had clear instructions about what was clean and what was unclean. There are those of us who are Christians, and we handle the dead things of this world deliberately. We touch them. We touch the unclean things. In 2 Corinthians 6:17, the Bible says, "Come out from among them and be separate, says the Lord. Do not touch what is unclean..."

People in Old Testament times understood what God was talking about in this chapter and chapters like it. It was something the Jewish people clearly understood. Similarly, a Christian is not to touch the unclean thing, represented by that dead body. Anytime we willfully, deliberately sin, at that moment our souls, our consciences, become unclean. We're unclean. We're dirty. We're defiled. We're polluted.

These deliberate acts of sin are the worst kind of sin. The Bible calls this presumptuous sin, and it carries with it the most severe penalty for the child of God. That's the reason the psalmist prayed, "Keep back Your servant also from presumptuous sins" (Psalm 19:13). Presumptuous sin is when you sin with your eyes wide open.

The next thing I want you to notice is not only the deliberate acts of sin described in Numbers 19:11, *but the defiling associations of sin.* If you look at Numbers 19:14-15, you read,

"This is the law when a man dies in a tent: All who come into the tent and all who are in the tent shall be unclean seven days; and every open vessel, which has no covering fastened on it, is unclean." In the Old Testament, they did not have all the technology and science we have today. But Moses did teach the people about health, hygiene, and safety—through the inspiration of the Holy Spirit. God gave to the people a sanitary code to keep them from contagion.

Even more than teaching personal health and hygiene, I want you to notice a great moral lesson from these verses. We need to beware of the defiling associations of sin. Here's a man who just simply might walk into the tent. He doesn't touch the dead body, but he's just in there. He walks around. He breathes the air. He's in the atmosphere. And God also says he shall be unclean. You see, there can still be defilement without actual contact.

Did you know that you and I don't have to deliberately sin to get defiled by this world?

- You can be watching television when defiling things come across the screen.

- You can be walking past a newsstand or magazine rack and notice sinful images.

- You can be scrolling through your phone or computer and be confronted by evil.

- You can be with friends and hear rude, suggestive, or off-color things.

- You can be minding your own business and be impacted by the sin that is all around you.

We live in a dirty old world. It's hard! We breathe the air, rub shoulders with, and live around so much filth and sin. It's hard to live without evil and unjust things in the air, in the tent, and where we are. Just by our very associations: newspapers, books, advertisements, humor—all of this will leave their mark upon us.

That's the reason we need to get away and get with our Lord and say, "Lord, give me a bath. Lord, make me clean, for I'm unclean."

Also, consider the truth that there are deceiving accidents of sin. If you look at Numbers 19:16, you will read, "Whoever in the open field touches one who is slain by a sword or who has died, or a bone of a man, or a grave, shall be unclean seven days." To me, this represents the sins that we, more or less, stumble into. Not presumptuous sin. Think about the image in this passage. Here's a man walking through a field after a battle when he stumbles over a dead body. Maybe there's just a small bone there and he touches that bone. Or perhaps unknown to him, he walks over a grassy covered grave, and he's unclean, too. The Bible calls him unclean.

What's God speaking about here? He's speaking not about the deliberate acts or the defiling associations, but the deceiving accidents of sin. These are those times in life when we don't intend to sin. It's not sin with our eyes wide open, but it just kind of creeps up on us. Without even realizing it, we're lusting, or we're filled with pride, or we are using harsh language. Without even planning on it, a covetous thought comes into our minds or concealed sins dull our spiritual perception. This is the reason we ought not only to pray the words of Psalm 19:13, "Keep back Your servant also from presumptuous sins," but we also ought to pray, "Search me, O God…and see if there is any wicked way in me…" (Psalm 139:23-24).

Honestly, I think it would surprise us to know how many times we've touched an unclean thing and not known it. I think it would surprise us to know how many graves we've walked over. Also, I think it would surprise us to know how many bones we've accidentally touched without knowing it.

God is talking about sin. He's not really talking about hygiene. He's talking about ceremonial uncleanness. He's talking about moral uncleanness, and He's saying that we need to be very careful, lest this vile world pollute us. Ultimately, God wants us to be clean.

The Consequences of an Unclean Conscience

Now, I want you to notice the consequences of an unclean conscience. What happens when we become unclean in the sight of God? First of all, when we become unclean in the sight of God, *we lose fellowship with others.*

Consider the words of Numbers 19:20, "But the man who is unclean and does not purify himself, that person shall be cut off from among the assembly…." In Bible days, being unclean was to be cut off from friends and family. In other words, they lost fellowship with their brothers and sisters in Christ. Sin separates the people of God. The sweetest thing that any church can ever have is fellowship. Where the Spirit of the Lord is there is fellowship. But it is sin that divides people. It is sinning that cuts people off. And when two people cannot get along, you mark it down, somebody has sinned.

May I say that again? When any two people can't get along together, somebody has sinned. Someone is unclean and needs to get right.

Also, another consequence of an unclean conscience is *the loss of freedom with God.* If you will look again at Numbers 19:20, you will read, "But the man who is unclean and does not purify himself, that person shall be cut off from among the assembly, because he has defiled the sanctuary of the LORD. The water of purification has not been sprinkled upon him; he is unclean."

When an unclean person prays, he or she defiles the sanctuary. When a man like this comes into the house of God, which in this particular time was the Old Testament tabernacle, and if he tries to come and worship with sin in his heart, it is an abomination to God. He has no freedom to worship. In Isaiah 59:1-2, the Bible says, "Behold, the LORD's hand is not shortened, that it cannot save; nor His ear heavy, that it cannot hear. But your iniquities have separated you from your God; and your sins have hidden His face from you, so that He will not hear."

A third consequence of living in sin is *the loss of fruitfulness in service*. In Numbers 19:22, we read, "Whatever the unclean person touches shall be unclean...." Not only is he unclean, but he pollutes everything else he touches. You see, if a person is not right with God, rather than ministering life when he ministers, he will minister death.

Did you know I'd pay $500.00 to have a soloist not sing if that soloist is not right with God? I'd pay even more than that to have a preacher not preach if he's not right with God. I'd rather have no preaching than preaching that comes from unclean lips. I'd rather have no teaching than teaching that comes from unclean lips. The Bible says repeatedly, talking about the sanctuary service, the temple service, and the tabernacle service, "Be clean, you who bear the vessels of the LORD" (Isaiah 52:11).

As a matter of fact, I know I'm not the smartest man in the world. Honestly, I don't even rank among those who are smart. But I've got enough sense never to stand in the pulpit with sin in my heart. And I hope to God I never do. More than that, I'd be mortally afraid before God, to stand on the stage, open this Bible, and try and preach knowing that I'd been handling unclean things. If my conscience was defiled and unclean, I could not preach at all. I want to be clean. I want to be pure. If I am unclean, I'll minister death, not life! Everything I touch will be unclean because I'm unclean.

That's why people should not take holy things in unholy hands. Rather than ministering life, they minister death. They may preach theologically correctly, they may sing perfectly, but there's no blessing. Oh, the people may clap and say, "That's good," but God doesn't work. Nobody's blessed. Nobody's saved. It is wood, hay, and stubble rather than gold and silver and precious stones.

Let's look again at Hebrews 9:14, "How much more shall the blood of Christ, who through the eternal Spirit offered Himself without spot to God, cleanse your conscience from dead works to serve the living God?"

Do you know why some churches never progress? Do you know why some Sunday school classes never grow and they're not blessed? Do you know why some people never win souls? Do you know why some peoples' prayers never get any higher than the lightbulbs? They work, but their works are dead works because they've got a dirty conscience. They're polluted. They don't have a clean conscience with God.

Paul told Timothy, "Now the purpose of the commandment is love from a pure heart, from a good conscience, and from sincere faith" (1 Timothy 1:5). Sincere faith and a good conscience…Those are the two things you need to fight your warfare.

The Cleansing of an Unclean Conscience

Let's go back once again to Numbers 19 as we think about the cleansing of an unclean conscience or the purging of a conscience. Notice the words of Numbers 19:1-5:

> Now the LORD spoke to Moses and Aaron, saying, "This is the ordinance of the law which the Lord has commanded, saying: 'Speak to the children of Israel, that they bring you a red heifer without blemish, in which there is no defect and on which a yoke has never come. You shall give it to Eleazar the priest, that he may take it outside the camp, and it shall be slaughtered before him; and Eleazar the priest shall take some of its blood with his finger, and sprinkle some of its blood seven times directly in front of the tabernacle of meeting. Then the heifer shall be burned in his sight: its hide, its flesh, its blood, and its offal shall be burned.'"

The cleansing agent was the heifer that was sacrificed. This heifer is a picture of Christ. Numbers 19:2 tells us that the heifer was to be without blemish and without defect. It also tells us that it could not be scarred by the yoke of sin. In Numbers 19:3, we are told that it would die outside the gate, outside the camp, just as Jesus died. In Numbers 19:5, we are told how this heifer was to be burned. This section of Scripture speaks of Jesus Christ who endured the fires of the wrath of God for us.

Then, in Numbers 19:4, we learn how this perfect sacrifice was offered. "Eleazar the priest shall take some of its blood with his finger, and sprinkle some of its blood seven times directly in front of the tabernacle of meeting." That verse speaks of the blood of Jesus Christ. This red heifer in perfection, an animal without defect or blemish, was a picture of the perfect Savior and our sacrifice for sin. So, the first thing I want to say about the cleansing agent is that the cleansing agent must be acceptable to God.

Secondly, I want to say the cleansing agent must be accessible to man. If you look at Numbers 19:9, you read, "Then a man who is clean shall gather up the ashes of the heifer, and store them outside the camp in a clean place; and they shall be kept for the congregation of the children of Israel for the water of purification; it is for purifying from sin."

God made a way for the people to be purified. In other words, God says, "You take the ashes of this red heifer that's been burned, put them in a pot, have a man carry them out to a clean spot, and set them there in that very clean spot. Then there'll be a time when those ashes can be mixed with water and brought back and be used to make the unclean clean." What does all of this represent? This pictures the atoning sacrifice of the Lord Jesus Christ forever deposited in Heaven, a clean place, for you and for me. Those ashes were evidence of the finished sacrifice; they were perpetually preserved for removal of daily sin and its pollution.

These ashes were not used for a person who had never been a Jew and had never been a part of the congregation. This is not talking about a person having his sins forgiven so he can be saved. This is talking about a saved person who, by deliberate acts of sin, or by defiling associations with sin, or by deceiving accidents of sin, needs to be cleansed. God said, "I'll make a provision."

In this section of Scripture, the heifer represented the Lord Jesus Christ. Those ashes represented the finished work of Calvary and a perpetual monument to the work of Calvary because the Bible says, "If we confess our sins, He is faithful and just to forgive us our sins and to cleanse us from all unrighteousness" (1 John 1:9).

A third thing I want you to see about the cleansing of an unclean conscience is that it is applied by faith. If you look in Numbers 19:17-18, you read:

And for an unclean person they shall take some of the ashes of the heifer burnt for purification from sin and running water shall be put on them in a vessel. A clean person shall take hyssop and dip it in the water, and sprinkle it on the tent, on all the vessels, on the persons who were there, or on the one who touched a bone, the slain, the dead, or a grave.

The cleansing process was clear and simple. The people would take ashes and running water and mix them together. Then, they would take the hyssop, which was a plant, just a little shrub, and put it down in this water of ashes. Finally, they would take this mixture and sprinkle it on the person who was unclean, the one who had touched a dead thing. Upon doing this, the Bible says, "then he will be clean."

Let's consider some of the symbolism here. What does the running water symbolize? Remember, the ashes symbolized the finished work of Calvary. That heifer is a picture of Christ. The running water symbolizes the Word of God. The Word of God is likened over and over in the Bible to water—the washing of water by the Word. What does the hyssop symbolize? The hyssop is a common shrub. This represents faith. It is the applying agent. You see, hyssop is a symbol of faith that applies the water and the blood. You just simply take faith (hyssop) and apply the water and the ashes to any sin, and you'll be clean.

Closing Thoughts on a Clean Conscience

This entire lesson has blessed my heart. I hope you have been encouraged as well. Perhaps you wonder, as you read, if I'm stretching the symbolism a little too far? You may say, "Brother Rogers, people can read the Bible and they see all kinds of strange things in it. Are you sure that's what that means?" To you I would say, "I'm really sure." You may answer, "Well, why are you so sure?" Let me show you as I close out this chapter.

The Bible is a wonderful book. It really is. The more I study it, I don't find hidden flaws; I find hidden beauties. I find little gems of truth that are written all over. I want to show you one of these gems. Let's look in Hebrews 9:11-14:

But Christ came as High Priest of the good things to come, with the greater and more perfect tabernacle not made with hands, that is, not of this creation. Not with the blood of goats and calves, but with His own blood He entered the

Most Holy Place once for all, having obtained eternal redemption. For if the blood of bulls and goats and the ashes of a heifer, sprinkling the unclean, sanctifies for the purifying of the flesh, how much more shall the blood of Christ, who through the eternal Spirit offered Himself without spot to God, cleanse your conscience from dead works to serve the living God?

You can't serve God if you don't have a clean conscience. But it's the blood of Jesus that makes your conscience clean. I thank God He has provided a perpetual sacrifice. I don't have to go around with sin on my soul. Yes, I sin every day. Yes, I have to ask God to forgive me. And sometimes, how my heart makes me ashamed, especially when I have to ask God to forgive me for the same things over and over again. But I thank God there's a pot full of ashes. I thank God there's a perpetual sacrifice. I thank God there's the running water. And I thank God there is the hyssop, the faith, so common, so available.

God has given all of us the measure of faith. We don't have to go around with a load of guilt on us. We don't have to walk around saying, "Unclean, unclean, unclean, unclean." Certainly, we will stumble into sin, get defiled by sin that we are often unaware of, and even, at times, choose to deliberately sin. However, I'm so glad that the Bible says in 1 John 1:9, "If we confess our sins, He is faithful and just to forgive us our sins and to cleanse us from all unrighteousness."

Let's pray together as we close this chapter:

Father, thank You for forgiveness and grace. Thank You for Your mercy and for providing a way for us to be cleansed. We are so grateful for Jesus and for His gift to us. May we keep short accounts and stay close to You and clean before You. We ask You to lead us not into temptation and deliver us from evil. Truly, it is our desire to live before You with a clean conscience. Amen.

CHAPTER THIRTEEN

Seven Feasts: Celebrating Jesus

"These seven feasts speak of all that God has done for you, and I'm
inviting you to come to the feast. Will you come?"
—Adrian Rogers

I n this final chapter about the tabernacle, let's take a look at some of
the Jewish festivals and feasts which add more context to our study.
Let's begin our review in Leviticus 23:4, "These are the feasts of the
LORD, holy convocations which you shall proclaim at their appointed
times."

Throughout time, the devil has tried to get us to think that God
is a cosmic killjoy, and that in order to be saved you have to put your
well-being and your happiness aside.

When Satan came into the Garden of Eden and crawled his slimy,
corroding path into the pages of history, he asked Eve a question. He
asked her, "Has God said that you shall not eat of every tree of the
garden?" Satan implied by this question, "Eve, you can't have any of
this." Friend, if you check the record in Genesis 2:16, you will read
where God said, "Of every tree in the garden you may freely eat." You
see, God had not said no to pleasure; He had said a resounding yes.
But the devil tried to twist things up for Eve.

The devil wants you also to think negatively about salvation. But
think about it: the cross is not in the form of a minus sign; it's in the
shape of a plus mark! Jesus didn't say, "I've come that you might have
death." Jesus said in John 10:10, "I have come that they may have life,
and that they may have it more abundantly." The Gospel is a feast,

not a funeral. God gave feasts to us. He tucked away in the Book of Leviticus—corresponding to the tabernacle worship—seven feasts that the Jews were to keep.

All of these feasts come in a very definite sequence. They are steps to glory. One follows the other, and each teaches a wonderful lesson. Looking at these will be like attending a sumptuous Gospel banquet, something for our enjoyment. God invites you to bring your appetite and to be satisfied and to feast on the fare He has provided in the Gospel. These feasts are first taught in the Old Testament, then they are amplified and explained in the New Testament. In the Old Testament the truth is enfolded; in the New Testament it is unfolded and revealed to us. Let's note the seven feasts of the Lord.

Feast Number One: The Passover Feast

The first feast is found in Leviticus 23:4-5: "These are the feasts of the LORD, holy convocations which you shall proclaim at their appointed times. On the fourteenth day of the first month at twilight is the LORD's Passover."

The Passover Feast speaks to us of salvation. You will remember the Passover was the night God delivered those ancient people from the land of Egypt. The Israelites went out underneath the blood of the Lamb into the land of Canaan. The blood of the lambs sprinkled on the doorpost represents the blood of the Lord Jesus Christ.

Look at Exodus 12. I want you to see very clearly that the Passover represents Christ dying on the cross for us. Notice the Bible says in Exodus 12:1-4:

> Now the LORD spoke to Moses and Aaron in the land of Egypt, saying, "This month shall be your beginning of months; it shall be the first month of the year to you. Speak to all the congregation of Israel, saying: 'On the tenth of this month every man shall take for himself a lamb, according to the house of his father, a lamb for a household. And if the household is too small for the lamb, let him and his neighbor next to his house take it according to the number of the persons; according to each man's need you shall make your count for the lamb.'"

A lamb is provided. And not just any kind of a lamb according to Exodus 12:5-6, which says, "Your lamb shall be without blemish, a male of the first year. You may take it from the sheep or from the goats. Now you shall keep it until the fourteenth day of the same month. Then the whole assembly of the congregation of Israel shall kill it at twilight."

A lamb. A perfect lamb. A slain lamb. When John the Baptist saw Jesus coming, he said, "Behold! The Lamb of God who takes away the sin of the world!" (John 1:29). The Passover feast pre-conditioned minds for a lamb—a suffering, sacrificial, sinless lamb that would die. Here is a picture of the Lord Jesus Christ. In Exodus 12:5-6, we see His perfection and His crucifixion. But I want you to notice that it is not enough for the lamb to die. Consider the words of Exodus 12:7, "And they shall take some of the blood and put it on the two doorposts and on the lintel of the house where they eat it." It's not enough that the blood be shed, but now the blood must be applied openly, publicly, unashamedly. By faith, it is appropriated.

God continues in Exodus 12:12-13, "For I will pass through the land of Egypt on that night, and will strike all the firstborn in the land of Egypt, both man and beast; and against all the gods of Egypt I will execute judgment: I am the LORD...And when I see the blood, I will pass over you..." Why? Because, as Hebrews 9:22 says, "without shedding of blood there is no remission" of sin.

Can you imagine the night of the Passover? A little Hebrew boy might be talking to his dad and say, "Dad, you know, everything Moses says comes true. He is God's prophet. Dad, don't you think we'd better get us a lamb and put the blood on the door posts? After all, I'm the first-born son. I've got more interest in this thing than anybody else."

And the dad says, "Son, we're going to do just exactly what Moses said." So, they got a perfect lamb. They kept it. They looked at it to make sure there's no spot, no blemish. The lamb is slain. The hyssop is dipped. The blood is applied.

And that night, the boy says, "Father, have we done everything the Lord told us to do?"

And the father said, "We've done it all, my son. Go to sleep." And that boy goes to sleep, and he sleeps well because he sleeps under the protection of the blood.

Now, imagine there's another Hebrew boy in another Hebrew home. He says to his dad in the house of Israel, "Dad, don't you think we'd better get us a lamb and make us a sacrifice?"

The dad answers, "Sure, son, we'll do that."

But this boy doesn't go to sleep. He wakes up about midnight and he hasn't gone to sleep yet. He says, "Dad, let's go out and check again. Is the blood on the door post? Have we done it just right?"

The dad answers, "Yes, son, we've done it right, just like God said. Go to sleep."

And about 2:00 a.m. he's tossing and turning. He said, "Dad, are you sure the death angel is not going to come by?"

The dad answers, "No, son, he's not going to come by."

Early in the morning the boy wakes up with bags under his eyes. The death angel has passed over, but not through. The boy is safe.

What's the difference between the two boys? Both boys are under the blood. But one of them is not enjoying it nearly like the other. This boy reminds me of so many of the worriers in our midst today. They are saved, but they don't enjoy the assurance of their salvation. Do you know the difference between the two boys? The blood makes all Christ-followers sure. The Lord can save us and give us that blessed wonderful assurance. However, too many believers are going to Heaven second class when they ought to be going first class, when they ought to be enjoying their wonderful salvation.

Now, I want to imagine a third boy that night in the land of Egypt. This is Pharaoh's son. He comes to his father, and he says, "Father, do you know there's some talk going on among the Hebrew people. They say that God has spoken to Moses, and God has said to Moses that there's a death angel coming through. And every first born in every family is going to be slain unless there's the blood of a lamb applied to the doorpost. And Moses has been batting pretty good. He's batting a thousand, as a matter of fact. Everything he says comes to pass. And, Father, don't you think we ought to get us a lamb and apply it to the doorpost?"

And Pharaoh says, "Son, I'm up to here with these Hebrews and their religion. I want you to know that we've got a god to cover everything in the land of Egypt. There's nothing you have to worry about. We've got a god of agriculture. We've got a god of sex. We've got a god of life. We've got a god of death. We've got a god for this and a god for that. And we've got the best priests that money can buy. And I've got guards. And we've got our religion. Son, don't you worry about that blood of the lamb stuff. Go to bed. You'll be all right."

The boy answers, "If you say so, Dad," and he goes to bed.

But that night there is a sound, a flash, a gasp, and Pharaoh's son is dead, for God said, "When I see the blood, I will pass over you."

You may ask, "Are you certain the Passover lamb they feasted upon represents the Lord Jesus?" I'm absolutely certain! The Bible says in 1 Corinthians 5:7b, "For indeed Christ, our Passover, was sacrificed for us." Christ, our Passover. Isn't it beautiful how God taught such a wonderful lesson so long ago in the Book of Leviticus and in Exodus chapter 12? Christ is our Passover.

And so, the first feast these Jews kept was the Feast of the Passover and it spoke of Christ, our salvation.

Feast Number Two: The Feast of Unleavened Bread

The second feast is the Feast of the Unleavened Bread. Look in Leviticus 23:6, "And on the fifteenth day of the same month is the Feast of Unleavened Bread to the LORD; seven days you must eat unleavened bread." Now, what does this speak of? If Passover speaks of Christ, our salvation, this feast speaks of Christ, our separation, or it speaks of the separated life.

You see, leaven, in the Bible, is always symbolic of sin. In order to cause a loaf of bread to rise, we add leaven to the mix. It's a process of fermentation that causes things to swell up and to rise, and it permeates that in which it's placed. God has used leaven in the Bible always as a symbol of sin. God says, first of all, there's the Feast of the Passover which is salvation. Then there is the Feast of Unleavened Bread, which speaks of separation. When we get saved, the Lord didn't save us in our sins; He came to save us *from* our sins.

The Bible tells us in Matthew 1:21, "…and you shall call His name JESUS, for He shall save His people from their sins." However, there are some folks who claim to be saved, and they just keep on living the same old life. Friend, they've got a rude awakening. If they haven't been changed, they haven't been saved. Of course, I don't mean you're going to be sinless, because you can't be sinless until the Lord raptures you. But I'll tell you there's going to be a difference.

Before I was saved, I was running toward sin. Now that I know Christ, I'm seeking to run away from sin. There is a difference. Christ is come into my heart and into my life, and nothing would make me happier to know that I would never sin again. That would just thrill me. I don't say, "Oh, thank God I'm once saved, always saved. Now I can sin all I want to." I sin more than I want to right now. I don't want to because the Bible teaches when we get saved, we're changed. The teaching is shown here in the Feast of Unleavened Bread.

Remember, Jesus said, "Take heed and beware of the leaven of the Pharisees and the Sadducees" (Matthew 16:6). Jesus also warns against the leaven of Herod (see Mark 8:15). The leaven of the Pharisees was legalism. The leaven of the Sadducees was modernism. The leaven of the Herodians was worldliness. But it all speaks of sin. Beware of leaven. Beware of sin. Once we get saved, we're to live a life separated from the habit of sin.

Do you know what the Jews would do back in this day? When they got ready for the Feast of Unleavened Bread, spring housecleaning would begin. They would scrub the floor. They would scrub the walls. They would get on a ladder and scrub the ceiling. They would take all the utensils in the house and boil them in water.

Then, they had a special little sharp-pointed tool, and they would go in every crack in the house and scrape every crack to make sure there's no leaven—not a speck of leaven in the house. As we would like to say, they went over that house with a fine-toothed comb.

Their houses were absolutely clean—spotlessly, scrupulously clean with no leaven in the house. They didn't eat leaven in the Passover and there was to be no leaven whatsoever in the house.

Once all of this cleaning was complete, they did a strange thing. They would take some leavened bread and bring it back into the house and hide it. They would hide some up in a corner over a rafter. They would hide little lumps of leaven all over the house. When the father would come home, he would hunt for the hidden leaven. He would take a candle after their dinner and go all over the house with a feather brush or wooden spoon looking for this leavened bread that had been hidden. The Jewish children would laugh and enjoy the entire game as they would watch their fathers search for the hidden leaven. As the father would find a bit of leavened bread, he would take it and put it on a handkerchief. He would find another piece and put it in the handkerchief until finally it was all gone—he had taken it all.

The children would just rejoice to see their father tracking down "sin" in the household. Can you imagine what an object lesson this was to little children? We want to be so certain there's nothing in our household that's wrong. We want to be so certain that not only are we under the blood, but also our lives are clean.

After the father had searched and found there was no more, he would pray a prayer like this: "All kinds of leaven that are in my possession, which I have not observed or removed, shall be null and counted as the dust of the earth." That is, he's saying, "God, I have done my best. If there's any leaven I haven't found, don't hold it against me." And the Lord wouldn't. Friend, the only sins you have to worry about confessing are those the Holy Spirit will show you when you honestly search. The Jewish father would say, "Now, any leaven that I've not observed or found shall be counted null and void and shall be as the dust of the earth." And then he would take that handkerchief of leavened bread and burn it. This was the Feast of Unleavened Bread.

What is the Lord telling us? He is telling us that we are to be clean, that we are to be separate from sin. It's not enough to be under the blood positionally. We must walk in cleanliness practically day by day. It is not enough to be separated from sin. That's the problem with too many people. We are not only supposed to be dead to the world; we are supposed to be alive unto God.

Feast Number Three: The Feast of the Firstfruits

The third feast is the Feast of the Firstfruits. Now, if the Feast of Passover spoke of our salvation, the Feast of the Firstfruits speaks of our sanctification.

In the land of Israel, still to this day, the first harvest that ripens is the barley harvest. The priest would go out to the fields and take a portion of the barley harvest when it was ready for harvesting. When it was ripe, he would take three handfuls of grain, three handfuls of barley, and bring them before the tabernacle of the Lord. After he had gone through the appropriate ritual, he would take these three bundles of barley together and wave them before the Lord, side to side. It's called the wave offering. It was like a military salute to the Lord. He's waving these things before the Lord.

What did that typify? First, it typified they were thanking God that He had given the harvest. But it was also saying, this is a picture of what everything else is going to be, and it all belongs to God.

This feast also speaks of Christ because the Bible says in 1 Corinthians 15:20, "Christ is risen from the dead, and has become the firstfruits of those who have fallen asleep." Christ is the firstfruits. This refers right back to this passage in Leviticus 23:9-14. Just like Christ is the Passover, Christ is also the firstfruits. If you want to know what all the harvest is going to be like, you need to look at the firstfruits. If you want to know what we are going to be like in the resurrection, you need to look at Jesus. We are going to be like Him! He is the pattern.

But not only is He the pattern; He's the promise that all the harvest belongs to Him. I belong to Him. You belong to Him. "… Christ the firstfruits, afterward those who are Christ's at His coming" (1 Corinthians 15:23). But, you see, the main teaching here is that we now belong to the Lord Jesus Christ.

Look at Romans 14:9 for a moment, "For to this end Christ died and rose and lived again, that He might be Lord of both the dead and the living." God owns it all. It's all His. We are His. The Feast of the Firstfruits speaks of the fact the entire harvest belongs to the Lord. I belong to Jesus. You belong to Jesus. He is the firstfruits. We are the harvest, and it all belongs to Him.

Feast Number Four: The Feast of Pentecost

The first feast speaks of salvation, the second feast speaks of separation, the third feast speaks of sanctification, and the fourth feast speaks of spirituality.

On the day of Pentecost, the Holy Spirit was poured out on that infant church. But God had illustrated that and had prophesied that back in Leviticus 23 when He taught them to have the Feast of Pentecost.

Now, it was not called the Feast of Pentecost in the Old Testament. It was called the Feast of Weeks. Pentecost is a New Testament term. "*Pente*" is the Greek word for fifty. So, this feast took place fifty days after Passover. There were seven weeks between the Passover Feast and the Feast of Pentecost. That's an easy one for us to see because it typifies the outpouring of the Holy Spirit. Look in Leviticus 23:15-17:

> And you shall count for yourselves from the day after the Sabbath, from the day that you brought the sheaf of the wave offering: seven Sabbaths shall be completed. Count fifty days to the day after the seventh Sabbath; then you shall offer a new grain offering to the LORD. You shall bring from your dwellings two wave loaves of two-tenths of an ephah. They shall be of fine flour; they shall be baked with leaven. They are the firstfruits to the LORD.

Now, this is not the Feast of the Firstfruits, but this is an offering of firstfruits. There is a difference. Remember the wave offering took place before the harvest. But this feast takes place at the end of the harvest. The first was of barley; the second was of wheat. The first was just grain; the second was loaves of bread. In addition, the first feast is coarse grain; the other is finely ground flour that makes loaves.

What does it all picture? It's a beautiful picture. Remember Jesus said in John 16:7, "Nevertheless I tell you the truth. It is to your advantage that I go away; for if I do not go away, the Helper will not come to you; but if I depart, I will send Him to you."

Sometimes believers wish they could have lived when Jesus lived, to have walked and talked with Him while He was leading His earthly ministry. But these were pre-Pentecostal disciples. Jesus said what we have is better than what they had. It is better. In fact, "It is to your advantage that I go away…" (John 16:7). It is better to have the Holy Spirit inside you than Christ beside you.

Remember this. Wheat's better than barley. Barley was a poor man's bread. Barley was coarse meal.

On Pentecost, what happened to that group of disciples in the Early Church? The Holy Spirit was poured out upon them. They were baptized with the Holy Spirit. The Spirit of God was poured out upon those disciples. They were no longer just a bunch of independent grains of wheat; they became one loaf. They became one body. The Bible says in 1 Corinthians 12:13a: "For by one Spirit we were all baptized into one body."

What is the significance of the two loaves? I think God is speaking both of Gentiles and Jews by the two loaves here. But I also think God is saying He wants to make us one. Do you remember the Jewish Pentecost in Acts 2? Then later on in Acts 10, the Holy Spirit was poured out upon the Gentiles the same way. Two loaves picturing Pentecost. The Gentile Pentecost; the Jewish Pentecost—two loaves becoming one loaf.

All of us are in the same loaf of bread. We're all mingled and mixed together. There's leaven among us; we are not perfect. However, there's no leaven in the wave offering, the unleavened bread. That pictures our Lord and His standard. But when we come in reality, we know that as long as we're in the flesh, if we say that we have no sin, we deceive ourselves and the truth is not in us.

What a wonderful illustration here of spirituality. Just as the Holy Spirit was poured out upon that infant Church and made them one, we see that pictured and typified here in the Feast of Pentecost.

Feast Number Five: The Feast of the Trumpets

Moving on, let's look at the fifth feast which is the Feast of the Trumpets. Look in Leviticus 23:23:

> Then the LORD spoke to Moses, saying, "Speak to the children of Israel, saying: 'In the seventh month, on the first day of the month, you shall have a sabbath-rest, a memorial of blowing of trumpets, a holy convocation. You shall do no customary work on it; and you shall offer an offering made by fire to the LORD.'"

Numbers 10 tells us about these trumpets. They were silver trumpets, and they were made of one solid piece of silver. These silver trumpets were to be blown at this feast. Why? The Bible tells us that when the trumpets were blown, an announcement was made. Trumpets were blown to gather people in an alarm, to gather people for worship, to gather people for rejoicing, to tell them to move out, and so on. The trumpets would speak to the house of Israel. Their purpose was to proclaim or to announce.

According to Numbers 10, there were two of these silver trumpets. Silver, as you recall from earlier chapters about the tabernacle construction, is symbolic of redemption. Here are silver trumpets that speak loudly of redemption.

There are two major times when you and I are going to hear the trumpet of the Lord or at least when people are going to hear the trumpet sounds. First of all, there is a trumpet for the Church, and that's the rapture trumpet.

In 1 Thessalonians 4:16, the Bible says, "For the Lord Himself will descend from heaven with a shout, with the voice of the archangel, and with the trumpet of God." You see, I really believe that's what the Feast of the Trumpets speaks about. First, you have Calvary, then you have Pentecost, and then you have this great harvest of souls. Then you have the trumpet that is for the rapture of the Church.

There is also a second trumpet. It's a trumpet for Israel. Look at Isaiah 18:3 to learn more about this trumpet. The Bible says, "All inhabitants of the world and dwellers on the earth: when he lifts up a banner on the mountains, you see it; and when he blows a trumpet, you hear it."

What's going to happen when the trumpet is blown? In Isaiah 18:7, we read, "In that time a present will be brought to the LORD of hosts from a people tall and smooth of skin, and from a people terrible from their beginning onward, a nation powerful and treading down, whose land the rivers divide—to the place of the name of the LORD of hosts, to Mount Zion." God is going now to gather these dispersed Jewish people back unto Himself. In Isaiah 27:13, the Bible says, "So it shall be in that day: the great trumpet will be blown; they will come, who are about to perish in the land of Assyria, and they who are outcasts in the land of Egypt, and shall worship the LORD in the holy mount at Jerusalem." God is not finished yet, friend!

The trumpets, to me, speak of the Second Coming. They speak of the rapture of the Church and the gathering of Israel. They speak of God's purposes yet in the future. And God tucked away a hint, a clue over here in the Book of Leviticus, as He talks about the Feast of the Trumpets.

Feast Number Six: The Day of Atonement

Next, let's look at the sixth feast which is the Day of Atonement. Notice in Leviticus 23:26-28:

> And the LORD spoke to Moses, saying: "Also the tenth day of this seventh month shall be the Day of Atonement. It shall be a holy convocation for you; you shall afflict your souls, and offer an offering made by fire to the LORD. And you shall do no work on that same day, for it is the Day of Atonement, to make atonement for you before the LORD your God."

On the Day of Atonement, the high priest took two goats. He would lay his hands on the head of one goat and confess the sins of the people on the head of that goat. This was called the scapegoat. Then that goat was led away into the wilderness and released, never to come back again.

And then the other goat was taken, the substitutionary goat, and he was slain and killed. His blood was offered to the Lord and sprinkled on the mercy seat. What a wonderful picture of the Lord Jesus Christ whose precious blood has carried away my sins into the land of God's forgetfulness, never to be brought up again. This day was called the "Day of Atonement."

The word "atonement" means "to cover." Our sins were not put away in the Old Testament. In the truest sense, sins were not forgiven in the Old Testament, not in the fullest sense. Men were not completely justified in the Old Testament. Their sins were simply covered. If these animals could have really made atonement, Jesus never would have come.

There was a covering until such a time as Jesus Christ, the Lamb of God, could come and die. The word "atonement" really means to cover in such a way that God and man can come together.

Now, why does this come after the feast that typifies the Rapture? Because even though we are under the blood of Jesus Christ now because the Passover Lamb has been slain for us and the blood has been applied to the doorposts of our hearts, we're still not what we ought to be. We're still not really truly at one with our Lord.

We have never really completely been made like Him and one with Him. That will not happen until the Rapture, and then that great atonement, that great oneness, will come when we will be like the Lord Jesus Christ, and we will be with the Lord Jesus Christ. Right now, we are His betrothed. We're the bride of Christ, but the marriage hasn't been consummated. In glory it will be consummated, no longer twain, but one flesh.

Just as a husband and wife become one in the consummation of the marriage, we, in a much loftier and higher and more spiritual sense, become the bride of Christ, at one with our Lord. Not just simply engaged, not just simply betrothed, but the two become one. There is an atonement.

So, first of all, there is salvation. There is separation. There is sanctification. There is spirituality. There is the second coming. And then there is solidarity. We become one with our Lord. We are one with Him throughout all eternity, and this is the Feast of Atonement.

Feast Number Seven: The Feast of Tabernacles

Finally, let's move on to the seventh feast which is the Feast of Tabernacles. If you look at Leviticus 23:33-34, you will see, "Then the LORD spoke to Moses, saying, "Speak to the children of Israel, saying: 'The fifteenth day of this seventh month shall be the Feast of Tabernacles for seven days to the LORD.'" Skip down to verse 40-41:

> And you shall take for yourselves on the first day the fruit of beautiful trees, branches of palm trees, the boughs of leafy trees, and willows of the brook; and you shall rejoice before the LORD your God for seven days. You shall keep it as a feast to the LORD for seven days in the year. It shall be a statute forever in your generations. You shall celebrate it in the seventh month.

The people went camping. Everybody would come to Jerusalem, and they would go out in the forest. They would cut palm branches and myrtle branches, and they would make a little hut, a little lean-to, or a little arbor. They called it a "booth" or a "tabernacle."

They cooked in it, and they slept in it. The kids could hardly wait for the Feast of the Tabernacles because all of the children would come. Of all of the feasts, this was the longest, most inclusive, most joyous feast. Truly, it was just a good time; the climax of all. It was the last of the seven feasts of the Lord.

And what does it speak of? Well, to me, it speaks of Heaven itself. The Feast of the Tabernacles really speaks of Christ, our sufficiency. When we get to Heaven, every need, every hunger will be met. The reason they had the Feast of the Tabernacles is that God was reminding them He had taken care of them when they lived in tents.

Remember when they wandered in the wilderness? For forty years, He said, "I fed you and I clothed you and I took care of you." Now, He's saying, "Look, if I could take care of you out there, I can take care of you now."

When my wife Joyce and I were first married, we were still in college. For all those years of college and seminary, we were young marrieds. I wanted Joyce to be able to stay at home to take care of our children (as this was her heart's desire). At times, it was challenging to be working, going to school, and helping to raise a family, but we made it through those years. God did it actually. I give Him the praise. But for seven years, we lived from hand to mouth, and it was God's hand to our mouth. That's the way we lived.

What was God saying to these Israelites? I believe He was saying, "Look people, if I took care of you out there in those booths, out there in those little tabernacles, when you were living in the brush arbors, if I took care of you then, I could take care of you now."

See, that's the idea. That's what the Feast of the Tabernacles was all about. It is so sweet and wonderful. Let me show you a couple of additional verses as we close out this chapter. Look in Hebrews 11:13-16a:

> These all died in faith, not having received the promises, but having seen them afar off were assured of them, embraced them and confessed that they were strangers and pilgrims on the earth. For those who say such things declare plainly that they seek a homeland. And truly if they had called to mind that country from which they had come out, they would

have had opportunity to return. But now they desire a better, that is, a heavenly country.

They wandered about, but there's a better country for them. Abraham looked for a city that had foundations, whose builder and maker is God.

Let's consider one final verse. Look in Revelation 21:3: "And I heard a loud voice from heaven saying, 'Behold, the tabernacle of God is with men, and He will dwell with them, and they shall be His people. God Himself will be with them and be their God.'"

God is saying, "I am the God who took care of you when you were in the wilderness, and now I'm going to tabernacle with you."

That's what the Feast of Tabernacles means. God who has provided will provide. It's kind of like our Lord's Supper which looks both ways. It looks back to Calvary, but it also looks forward to the second coming of Jesus.

The Feast of Tabernacles looked back to the wilderness, but it looked forward. God was saying, "As I have provided, I will provide; as I have been faithful, I will be faithful." And there's coming a day when God Himself is going to tabernacle with us. What a feast that will be—the longest, most joyous, most all-inclusive feast.

Closing Thoughts About the Feasts

Jesus said the Kingdom of Heaven is like a man that made a great feast. He went out and invited those that were invited to come to the feast. And one man said, "I ask you to have me excused" (Luke 14:18). That was the worst prayer that was ever offered because it's always answered.

Now, I'm God's messenger boy, and I'm coming with an invitation to the King's banquet. Seven feasts. Seven is the number of perfection. These seven feasts speak of all that God has done for you, and I'm inviting you to come to the feast. Will you come?

Let's pray together as we close:

Father, would You help us to celebrate the feasts with You? Thank You for these wonderful pictures of Your goodness and Your faithfulness to us. May we come to Your feast. May we join You at the table. May we enjoy our relationship with You more every day. Because of Jesus. Amen.

OTHER RESOURCES

Remember and Share

Use this QR code to access and download a PDF infographic that will remind you of the structure, the artifacts, and the spiritual treasures pointing to Jesus you have discovered in this book about the Old Testament tabernacle. Use it to remember what you've learned and to share God's story with others.

Listen and Enjoy

Want to "hear" Jesus in unexpected places? You can listen to Adrian Rogers' audio messages from which this book was compiled. You'll feel like you've found a knowledgeable, biblically sound, and entertaining tour guide to take you through one of the most fascinating places in spiritual history.

The Tabernacle

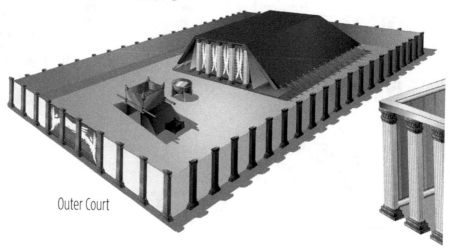

Outer Court

Brazen Altar

Bronze Laver

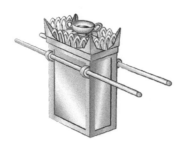

Altar of Incense

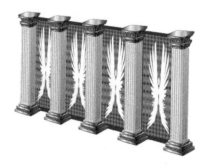

Veil to the Holy of Holies

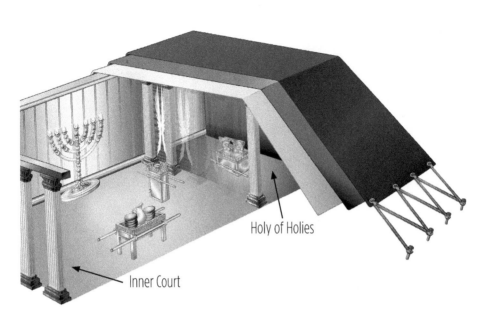

Holy of Holies

Inner Court

Golden Lampstand

Table of Showbread

The Mercy Seat

The Ark of the Covenant

Priests' Attire

ADDITIONAL TITLES BY ADRIAN ROGERS, JOYCE ROGERS & LOVE WORTH FINDING MINISTRIES

Published by Innovo Publishing LLC

1. *25 Days of Anticipation: Jesus . . . The Fulfillment of Every Heart's Longing*
2. *A Family Christmas Treasury*
3. *Adrianisms: The Collected Wit and Wisdom of Adrian Rogers*
4. *Believe in Miracles but Trust in Jesus*
5. *Discover Jesus: The Author and Finisher of our Faith*
6. *Foundations for Our Faith: A 3-Volume Bible Study of Romans*
7. *God's Hidden Treasures*
8. *God's Wisdom is Better than Gold*
9. *Good Morning, Lord: Starting Each Day with the Risen Lord (a 365 Day Devotional)*
10. *His Story: God's Purpose and Plans from Genesis to Revelation*
11. *Revelation Study Guide (2 Volumes)*
12. *Standing for Light and Truth: Living with Integrity to Shine God's Light in a World Going Dim*
13. *The Music of Marriage*
14. *The Passion of Christ and the Purpose of Life*
15. *The Power of His Presence*

* BY JOYCE ROGERS *

16. *Therefore, I Hope In Him*
17. *Chosen to be a Minister's Wife*
18. *Behold*

CPSIA information can be obtained
at www.ICGtesting.com
Printed in the USA
LVHW081905300922
729642LV00003BA/3